Financial Stress to Inevitable success

Table of Contents

Introduction: Why This Book? Why Now? 1
    It's Never Too Late to Start 2
    Why This Book Is Different 3
    What You Can Expect 4

Part 1: Understanding Your Financial Reality 5
    Broke AF: The Paycheck-to-Paycheck Life 5
    Swipe Right on Regret: The Credit Card Conundrum 10
    Assets vs Liabilities: The Tinder Edition 16
    Money Myths: Lies You've Been Spending On 19
    Myth #1: You need a six-figure income to save or invest. 20
    Myth #2: Debt is a necessary part of life. 21
    Myth #3: Renting is throwing money away. 21
    Myth #4: Budgeting means giving up all the fun. 21
    Myth #5: You can always make up for lost time later. 22
    Myth #6: Buying in bulk always saves money. 22
    Myth #7: You should always prioritize paying off debt over investing. 22
    Myth #8: More income automatically means more wealth. 23
    Myth #9: You need to know everything about investing before you start. 23
    Myth #10: Financial success is about luck. 23

Part 2: Building a Strong Financial Foundation 25
    Budget Like a Boss (Without Crying) 25

Emergency Funds: The Financial First-Aid Kit 28

The Debt Detox: Breaking Up with Bad Habits 33

Maximizing Your Pension: Planting the Seeds for Retirement 37

Ensure You're Not Leaving Free Money on the Table 40

Understanding your pension fund 43

The Long-Term Impact of Maximizing Your Pension 44

Part 3: Growing Wealth for the Future 46

Investing: Let's Make Money Make Money 46

Why Investing Matters 46

The Basics of Investing 47

Types of Investments 48

How to Get Started 51

The Power of Patience 52

Compound Interest: The Snowball Effect 54

Multiple Income Streams: Beyond the 9-to-5 58

Part 4: Reaching Financial Freedom 65

Breaking Free from Golden Handcuffs: The Exit Plan 65

Your Financial Freedom Plan: GPS to Your Goals 70

Part 5: Navigating Taxation and Maximizing Savings 73

Taxes Demystified: Don't Let the Brackets Fool You 73

Capital Gains Tax in the UK 75

USA Tax 76

How Understanding Taxes Can Help You Keep More of Your Money 78

Part 6: Securing Long-Term Stability Insurance..........................81
   Protecting Your Wealth: Insurance and Safeguards............................81
   Generational Wealth: Building a Legacy 88
   Strategic Investments: Building a Solid Foundation............................90
   Wills, Trusts, and Estate Planning: Protecting Your Legacy.............91
   Minimizing Tax Burden: A Critical Strategy...93
   The Human Element: Values and Knowledge......................................98
   Sustaining Prosperity Across Generations..99

Part 7: Beyond Financial Success 101
   Legacy and Giving Back: Leaving More Than Breadcrumbs 101
   Mindset Maintenance: Keeping the Hustle Alive 110

Part 8: Investing in Yourself 116
   Buying Knowledge: Education and Mentorship................................116

Part 9: Taking Action and Staying Disciplined.........................127

Part 10: Thriving in the Digital Financial Era...........................131
   Staying Ahead in the Digital Age..131
   Cybersecurity and Protecting Your Finances 131
   Adapting to Digital Finance 133

Conclusion: Your Journey Ahead - Time to Level Up 136

Conclusion: Thank You and Looking Ahead............................143

Disclaimer

This book is intended for informational and educational purposes only. The strategies, tips, and concepts shared here are based on the author's personal experiences and research. They should not be construed as financial advice or a recommendation to buy, sell, or hold any financial products or investments.

The information in this book is not a substitute for professional financial advice. Readers are encouraged to seek the assistance of a qualified financial advisor or other professional before making any financial decisions. The author and publisher are not responsible for any financial outcomes resulting from the application of the information provided in this book.

Introduction: Why This Book? Why Now?

Personal finance often feels like a mystery—a maze of terms, calculations, and strategies that seem impossible to navigate without a formal education or a career in finance. Many people feel stuck, unsure of how to manage their money or build wealth, thinking it's too late to start. This book was written to change that belief.

I didn't come from a finance background. My career began in cybersecurity, and I've never worked in the financial industry. Yet, over the past five years, from the age of 18 to 23, I taught myself everything there is to know about personal finance. It wasn't easy, and it didn't happen overnight. I grew up in East London, in a household that was sometimes middle class but often lower class during harder times. I know what it's like to go without certain things.

In my younger years, after leaving school, I fell into the same cycle many people experience: living paycheck to paycheck. Every month, I worked hard, spent whatever I earned, and repeated the process. I wasn't saving. I wasn't investing. I wasn't thinking about the future. I was just surviving. Around me, I saw friends and family struggling financially, living the same way. That realization hit me hard—I knew I had to change something. I wanted more than just getting by. I wanted to create a better life for myself.

That's when I made the decision to go all-in on learning. I poured my energy into computers, a passion I'd always had, and eventually joined a fantastic cybersecurity team that taught me a great deal. I climbed the corporate ranks, gaining skills and confidence along the way. But as I built my career, I also knew that financial success couldn't come from just earning a paycheck, no matter how good the job. So, I started teaching myself everything I could about personal finance.

I didn't have anyone guiding me. I didn't attend seminars, take expensive courses, or graduate from a top university. In fact, I went to a regular university in London and a state school before that. I didn't grow up with financial literacy, nor did I come from a culture that valued entrepreneurship. Success, as it was defined where I grew up, meant getting a stable job and working hard. The idea of building wealth, starting a business, or investing seemed like something for "other people"—not for me, not for my neighbors.

But I refused to accept that narrative. Through trial and error, countless hours of reading, and relentless determination, I went from knowing nothing about investing to building a large investment portfolio. I learned how to budget, save, and grow my money. Along the way, I realized how many people were in the same position I had been in—struggling, uninformed, and stuck in financial stress. That's why I wrote this book: to inspire and teach others that personal finance doesn't have to be as complicated as it seems.

It's Never Too Late to Start

One of the most common misconceptions I've encountered is the belief that it's too late to take control of your finances. Many older individuals feel that they've missed their chance to start investing, build wealth, or pursue side hustles. I want to be clear: that couldn't be further from the truth.

Some of the most successful business owners and entrepreneurs started later in life. Colonel Sanders founded KFC in his 60s. Vera Wang didn't become a fashion designer until her 40s. The timeline for success isn't set in stone. Whether you're 25 or 65, the principles of personal finance remain the same: budgeting, saving, investing, and creating opportunities. It's never too late to learn these skills, and it's never too late to change your financial future.

This belief in financial literacy being for everyone is one of the core messages of this book. I believe that everyone, regardless of their background, deserves access to the knowledge and tools that can help them achieve financial freedom. Unfortunately, these lessons are rarely taught in schools. Most of us leave the education system knowing how to calculate the area of a triangle but clueless about how to balance a budget or invest for retirement. That gap in our education leaves many people at a disadvantage, struggling unnecessarily with financial decisions.

Why This Book Is Different

I'm not a financial guru. I'm not here to overwhelm you with jargon or make you feel like you need to be an expert to succeed. This book is designed to simplify personal finance, breaking it down into straightforward, actionable steps that anyone can follow. My goal is to show you that financial success isn't reserved for the elite or the highly educated—it's achievable for anyone willing to learn and take action.

Through this book, I'll share everything I've learned, from my early struggles living paycheck to paycheck to building a thriving investment portfolio. I've made mistakes, and I'll be honest about them because I believe there's as much value in learning what not to do as there is in learning the right steps to take.

You'll find strategies for managing debt, creating a budget, and building an emergency fund. You'll learn how to start investing, even if you have limited resources, and how to grow your wealth over time. And you'll discover ways to create additional income streams, whether through side hustles or passive income opportunities.

What You Can Expect

This book is for everyone, whether you're just starting out or looking to improve your current financial situation. If you've ever felt overwhelmed by money matters, unsure of where to start, or stuck in a cycle of financial stress, this book is for you. My hope is that by the time you finish, you'll feel empowered to take control of your finances and inspired to create the life you want.

Remember, it's not about where you start—it's about where you're headed. Whether you're climbing out of debt, building your first savings account, or exploring investment opportunities, every step forward is progress.

Let's take that journey together.

Part 1: Understanding Your Financial Reality

Broke AF: The Paycheck-to-Paycheck Life

Living paycheck to paycheck isn't just a financial struggle—it's an emotional and psychological burden that permeates every aspect of life. It's a constant state of uncertainty, where even minor unexpected expenses feel like catastrophic events. For millions of people, this cycle isn't just a phase but a way of life, one that breeds stress, anxiety, and a sense of helplessness. The good news? It doesn't have to be permanent. Understanding the dynamics of paycheck-to-paycheck living and taking intentional steps can help break the cycle.

The paycheck-to-paycheck life often begins innocently. You start earning, covering your expenses, and treating yourself to small rewards. But as your expenses grow, your financial cushion shrinks. Unexpected costs like a car repair, a medical bill, or even a missed paycheck can send you scrambling. Before you know it, the balance between income and expenses is so tight that there's nothing left at the end of the month. It's a precarious existence, one where financial stability feels like a pipe dream. Yet, this situation doesn't develop overnight—it's often the result of years of choices, circumstances, and systemic barriers.

This lifestyle isn't just about poor financial choices—it's often a result of systemic issues. Stagnant wages, rising costs of living, and a lack of financial education all play a role. Many people grow up without learning basic financial skills, like budgeting, saving, or understanding interest rates. Without these tools, it's easy to fall into a cycle of spending every penny you earn just to keep up. Over time, this becomes a way of life, ingrained and seemingly unavoidable.

But the paycheck-to-paycheck life takes more than your money; it takes your peace of mind. Every decision becomes a trade-off. Do you pay the electric bill or buy groceries? Do you put off a necessary car repair and risk bigger problems later? These choices create a mental load that's hard to bear. Over time, the stress compounds, affecting your relationships, your health, and your ability to focus on anything beyond immediate needs. This perpetual anxiety can even lead to feelings of inadequacy or hopelessness, as if breaking free is impossible.

Breaking this cycle starts with a mindset shift. The first step is to understand where your money is going. This isn't about judgment or guilt; it's about clarity. Imagine your finances as a puzzle. You can't solve it unless you can see all the pieces. Start by tracking your expenses for a month. Write down every purchase, no matter how small. By the end of the month, you'll have a clear picture of your spending habits and areas where you might be able to cut back. Awareness is the foundation of change.

The next step is to create a budget, but not just any budget. It needs to be realistic and flexible. Budgets often fail because they're too restrictive, leaving no room for fun or unexpected expenses. A good budget accounts for your fixed costs (like rent and utilities), your variable costs (like groceries and transportation), and your savings goals. It also includes a category for discretionary spending, so you don't feel deprived. Flexibility within a budget is essential to keep it sustainable—and to avoid the frustration of constantly "failing" at sticking to a rigid plan.

Once you've created a budget, the goal is to create a gap between your income and your expenses. Even if it's just a small amount at first, this gap is what allows you to start saving and building an emergency fund. An emergency fund is crucial for breaking the paycheck-to-paycheck cycle. It acts as a financial buffer, allowing you to cover unexpected expenses without derailing your budget or resorting to credit cards. This gap, no matter how small, becomes the foundation of your financial stability, giving you a sense of control over your money rather than feeling controlled by it.

Think of an emergency fund as your personal safety net—a cushion that softens the blow of life's unpredictable moments. Without it, even minor setbacks like a flat tire, a sudden medical expense, or a temporary loss of income can spiral into larger financial crises. But with an emergency fund in place, you gain not only financial security but also peace of mind. You're no longer forced to rely on high-interest credit cards or borrow money from friends and family to make ends meet. This relief can have a profound impact on your mental well-being, reducing the stress and anxiety that often accompany financial instability.

Building an emergency fund might seem daunting, especially if money is already tight. However, it's important to start small and remain consistent. Begin by setting aside even a few pounds each week. Over time, these small contributions add up. Automating your savings—by transferring a set amount from your paycheck into a separate savings account—can make the process effortless. As your financial situation improves, you can gradually increase the amount you save, ultimately working toward a goal of three to six months' worth of living expenses.

An emergency fund not only provides a safety net but also shifts your mindset. It empowers you to approach financial hiccups with confidence rather than panic. When an unexpected expense arises, you can address it directly and move on, rather than letting it derail your entire budget. Over time, this sense of preparedness builds resilience, helping you stay on track with your broader financial goals. Even a modest emergency fund can transform how you navigate life's challenges, giving you the stability to focus on building a brighter, more secure future.

Another critical step is to tackle debt. For many people, debt is the anchor that keeps them stuck in the paycheck-to-paycheck cycle. High-interest debts, like credit cards or payday loans, can eat up a significant portion of your income, leaving little room for anything else. The first step in tackling debt is to stop accumulating more. This might mean cutting up your credit cards, saying no to new loans, or temporarily cutting back on non-essential spending. The psychological impact of confronting debt head-on cannot be underestimated—it shifts the narrative from helplessness to empowerment.

Once you've stopped the bleeding, you can focus on paying down what you owe. There are two popular strategies for tackling debt: the snowball method and the avalanche method. The snowball method involves paying off your smallest debts first, giving you quick wins and a sense of progress. The avalanche method focuses on paying off debts with the highest interest rates first, saving you money in the long run. Both methods work; the best one is the one you're most likely to stick with. The satisfaction of reducing debt fuels further motivation, making long-term goals feel attainable.

As you start to gain control of your finances, you'll notice something amazing: your mindset will begin to shift. What once felt like an impossible situation will start to feel manageable. You'll begin to see opportunities to improve your financial situation, whether it's picking up a side hustle, negotiating a raise, or finding ways to save on everyday expenses. The possibilities grow as the weight of paycheck-to-paycheck living lifts—and this sense of possibility is empowering in itself.

One of the most important lessons in breaking the paycheck-to-paycheck cycle is learning to delay gratification. Our culture often glorifies instant rewards—the idea that you should treat yourself now and worry about the consequences later. But true financial freedom comes from being able to make intentional choices. It's not about depriving yourself but about prioritizing the things that matter most. Instead of buying something on impulse, take a moment to ask yourself:

Does this align with my goals? Is this worth delaying my progress toward financial stability?

Breaking free from the paycheck-to-paycheck life isn't easy. It requires patience, discipline, and a willingness to confront uncomfortable truths about your financial habits. But it's worth it. Imagine a life where you don't have to stress about unexpected expenses, where you can save for the future, and where you have the freedom to make choices based on what you want, not just what you can afford. This vision may seem distant at first, but every small step brings it closer to reality.

The journey won't be perfect. There will be setbacks and challenges along the way—unexpected expenses, moments of doubt, and even times when progress feels slow. But every small step you take—whether it's tracking your expenses, building your emergency fund, or paying down debt—brings you closer to financial freedom. Each decision to make a smarter financial choice is a vote for the future you want, and over time, those small choices compound into significant change.

Breaking free from the paycheck-to-paycheck cycle is like breaking out of a constricting mold that has limited your potential. It's a powerful transformation that not only reshapes your finances but also rewires your mindset. Imagine waking up each day with the confidence that you can handle whatever life throws at you, knowing that your financial future is no longer dictated by stress or scarcity. This newfound freedom allows you to focus on goals and dreams that once felt out of reach, like traveling, pursuing a passion project, or even just enjoying life without the constant weight of financial worry.

And once you break free, you'll never want to go back. The relief of knowing you have control over your money and the ability to plan for the future far outweighs the temporary gratification of overspending. This transformation is not only financial; it's a shift in how you approach life. You'll find yourself more resilient in the face of challenges, more confident in your ability to make decisions, and more motivated to continue building the life you envision. It's about stepping into a mindset where you see yourself as capable and deserving of financial stability and success, no matter where you started. The belief that your future is in your hands becomes a driving force, empowering you to create a life of abundance, security, and fulfillment.

Swipe Right on Regret: The Credit Card Conundrum

Credit cards are among the most deceptively alluring financial tools in the modern world. They promise convenience, flexibility, and rewards—a world of instant gratification where your desires are only a swipe away. Need a new outfit? Swipe. Want to book that spontaneous weekend getaway? Swipe. The appeal of credit cards is deeply ingrained in modern consumer culture, where the ability to pay later feels empowering, almost like having a safety net that stretches beyond the limits of your bank account. But behind their shiny exterior lies a financial trap that millions of people fall into every year. Without careful management, credit cards can transform from a tool of convenience into a source of financial strain, leading to a cycle of debt that is incredibly hard to escape.

The psychological allure of credit cards is one of their greatest dangers. When you use cash, the act of handing over money creates a tangible sense of loss, which helps curb impulsive spending. Credit cards, however, detach you from the immediate reality of your expenses. A simple swipe or tap makes transactions feel painless, encouraging you to spend more than you might otherwise. This detachment often leads to a "out of sight, out of mind" mentality, where the growing balance on your card doesn't feel real until the bill arrives—by which point, it may already be unmanageable.

Adding to the problem is the illusion of affordability. Credit cards give you the ability to buy things you technically can't afford, breaking down significant purchases into smaller, seemingly manageable payments. While this may feel like financial flexibility, it often leads to overextending your budget. A £500 shopping spree might not feel overwhelming when spread out over months of minimum payments, but the reality is that interest accumulates quickly, turning that purchase into a far more expensive commitment than you initially realized.

What's worse, the minimum payment system is designed to keep you in debt. Paying only the minimum amount due often covers little more than the interest on your balance, leaving the principal amount barely touched. This can extend the life of your debt indefinitely. For example, a £500 balance at an 18% interest rate could take over five years to pay off if you stick to minimum payments—and you'd end up paying nearly double the original amount. This compounding debt traps countless individuals in a cycle where progress feels impossible, making credit card balances a source of persistent stress and anxiety.

Credit card companies are well aware of the human tendency to prioritize short-term gratification over long-term consequences, and they capitalize on it. Rewards programs, cashback offers, and exclusive perks are marketed as incentives to use your card more frequently. While these benefits can be enticing, they often come at a cost. For every point or cashback pound you earn, you risk accruing interest charges that far outweigh the rewards. The psychological impact of these programs can be powerful, leading many people to justify unnecessary spending in the name of earning points or rewards.

Beyond the financial implications, the emotional toll of credit card debt is profound. Carrying a balance can create a constant undercurrent of stress and guilt. You might find yourself dreading the arrival of your monthly statement, avoiding calls from creditors, or losing sleep over how to make ends meet. This stress can seep into other areas of your life, affecting relationships, work performance, and even physical health. Arguments about money are one of the leading causes of tension in relationships, and the weight of financial uncertainty can erode self-confidence and mental well-being.

The consequences of unchecked credit card use extend far beyond individual finances. Credit card debt can act as a barrier to achieving larger financial goals, such as saving for a home, investing for the future, or building an emergency fund. It narrows your options, forcing you to allocate resources toward interest payments rather than opportunities for growth or security. Over time, this can create a sense of stagnation, where it feels impossible to move forward despite your best efforts.

However, credit cards are not inherently bad. When used responsibly, they can offer benefits such as fraud protection, convenience, and even rewards that enhance your financial life. The key is to use them as a tool rather than a crutch. This begins with a clear understanding of how they work and a commitment to setting boundaries. For instance, treat your credit card like cash: only charge what you can afford to pay off in full each month. By avoiding carrying a balance, you eliminate the risk of falling into the debt trap and can take advantage of the perks without paying for them in interest.

Another essential step is to educate yourself about the terms and conditions of your credit cards. Understand how interest rates are calculated, what fees you might incur, and how your credit limit affects your overall financial health. Knowledge is power, and being informed allows you to make decisions that align with your long-term goals rather than impulsive desires.

If you're already in credit card debt, the path to recovery starts with acknowledgment and action. Begin by assessing your balances, interest rates, and minimum payments. Create a plan to tackle your debt using strategies like the snowball method, which focuses on paying off the smallest balances first to build momentum, or the avalanche method, which targets the highest-interest debts to save money over time. Choose the approach that feels most achievable for you and stay consistent. Progress, no matter how small, builds confidence and momentum.

The credit card conundrum begins with the illusion of affordability. When you swipe your card, it doesn't feel like spending real money. There's no immediate impact on your bank account, no cash leaving your wallet. It's a mental trick that makes it easy to overspend. But what starts as a harmless convenience can quickly snowball into a significant financial burden. That purchase you barely thought about suddenly becomes a long-term obligation as interest rates add up and payments linger. Credit cards offer ease, but at a steep hidden cost.

Debt on credit cards builds stealthily. The minimum payment option, which might seem like a lifeline, is actually a trap designed to keep you in debt for as long as possible. By paying only the minimum, most of your payment goes toward interest, not the principal balance. This means that even small purchases can take years to pay off and cost you significantly more than their original price. For example, a £500 purchase at an 18% interest rate could take over five years to pay off if you only make minimum payments—and you'd end up paying almost double the original amount. The long-term consequences of such practices are often underestimated, but they can derail your financial health for years.

Credit card companies are not shy about taking advantage of human psychology. They entice you with rewards programs, cashback offers, and exclusive perks, all designed to encourage spending. These benefits, while tempting, often come at a price. For every point or cashback pound you earn, the interest you pay on an unpaid balance easily outweighs those rewards. The allure of these perks can push people into spending more than they can afford, creating a cycle where the benefits feel like justification for increasing debt. It's a game stacked in favor of the credit card companies.

The emotional toll of credit card debt is just as significant as the financial cost. Carrying a balance can create a constant undercurrent of stress, guilt, and anxiety. You might find yourself dreading the arrival of your monthly statement, avoiding calls from creditors, or losing sleep over how to make ends meet. The pervasive worry about how to handle mounting debt can drain your mental energy and undermine your confidence. Over time, the burden of credit card debt can lead to feelings of shame and helplessness, trapping you in a cycle that's hard to break.

The impact of credit card debt doesn't stop at your finances. It can seep into other areas of your life, affecting relationships, work productivity, and even your physical health. Arguments about money are one of the leading causes of stress in relationships, and financial worries can make it difficult to focus on long-term goals or opportunities. The cost of credit card debt isn't just monetary; it's emotional and social, too.

So how do you avoid the credit card conundrum? The first step is to approach credit cards with a clear plan and strict boundaries. Credit cards are tools, and like any tool, they can be helpful or harmful depending on how you use them. This requires honesty about your spending habits and a commitment to financial discipline. Treat your credit card like cash: if you don't have the money to cover the expense immediately, don't charge it. Avoid carrying a balance at all costs, as the interest will eat away at your financial stability over time.

Another crucial step is to educate yourself about the terms and conditions of your credit cards. Many people are unaware of how interest rates are calculated, how late fees accrue, or how minimum payments are structured. This lack of knowledge gives credit card companies the upper hand. By understanding how your card works, you can make more informed decisions and avoid falling into common traps.

If you're already in credit card debt, it's important to tackle it head-on with a strategy. Start by listing all your balances, interest rates, and minimum payments. Two popular methods for paying off debt are the snowball method and the avalanche method. The snowball method involves paying off your smallest debts first to build momentum and confidence, while the avalanche method targets the highest-interest debts to save money over time. Choose the approach that feels most achievable for you and stick to it. Progress, no matter how small, is still progress.

Building an emergency fund is another critical step in breaking free from reliance on credit cards. An emergency fund serves as a safety net for unexpected expenses, reducing the need to charge emergencies to a credit card. Even a modest fund of £500 to £1,000 can make a significant difference. This fund provides peace of mind and allows you to handle unforeseen financial hiccups without adding to your debt.

Lastly, consider shifting your mindset about credit. Credit cards are not a measure of your financial success or worth; they are simply tools that require discipline and responsibility. Use them wisely, and they can work to your advantage. But remember, no rewards program or cashback offer is worth the stress and long-term costs of unmanageable debt. Financial freedom begins with taking control of your spending and prioritizing your financial health over short-term indulgences.

Breaking free from the credit card conundrum requires awareness, intention, and persistence. It's not always easy, but the rewards are worth it. Imagine a life where your paycheck isn't swallowed up by interest payments, where you can use credit as a tool instead of a crutch, and where you have the confidence to make financial decisions that align with your long-term goals. That life is within reach—one intentional choice at a time.

Assets vs Liabilities: The Tinder Edition

Imagine your financial life as a dating app. Each financial decision you make is like swiping left or right, deciding what belongs in your life and what doesn't. Assets are the keepers—the ones that bring value, stability, and long-term benefits. Liabilities, on the other hand, are the red flags. They're flashy, tempting, and often fun in the short term, but ultimately, they drain your resources and leave you feeling regretful. It's time to refine your swiping habits and start choosing financial keepers over red-flag decisions.

Assets are the financial equivalents of a great match. They work for you, even when you're not paying attention. Think of them as the dependable, growth-oriented partners of your financial world. These could be investments that increase in value over time, like stocks, bonds, or real estate. They might also include things like an education or skillset that boosts your earning potential, or a healthy savings account that provides a sense of security. Think of your assets as the matches that make your future brighter and your financial life more stable—the ones you introduce to your family and friends with pride.

Liabilities, however, are the financial bad dates. They seem appealing at first—that brand-new car you've been eyeing, the designer wardrobe you bought on credit, or the subscription services you forgot about but keep paying for. These are the decisions that look good in the moment but ultimately leave you drained and regretting the choice. The worst part? They often disguise themselves as assets, making it harder to spot the red flags until it's too late. A liability can masquerade as an exciting fling, but it's one that often overstays its welcome and leaves you with emotional and financial baggage.

Here's the secret to distinguishing between the two: Ask yourself if this financial decision will bring long-term value or if it's simply a temporary thrill. Assets appreciate over time or provide a return on investment. Liabilities, on the other hand, depreciate or cost you more money in the long run. For example, a car can be both an asset and a liability. If it's reliable, fuel-efficient, and helps you earn an income or manage essential errands efficiently, it's an asset. However, if it's a high-end luxury vehicle with sky-high payments, hefty insurance premiums, and significant maintenance costs that eat into your budget, it's a liability in disguise. Much like a dating profile with only glamorous pictures, you need to dig deeper to see the true cost of the relationship.

To truly assess whether something is an asset or liability, think beyond the surface appeal. For example, consider a new gadget purchase. While it might be exciting and trendy, ask yourself: Will this device genuinely enhance my productivity or simplify my life in a way that adds long-term value? Or is it simply a fleeting desire fueled by marketing? Similarly, when evaluating financial opportunities, consider their impact on your net worth over time. Is it a positive addition that compounds and grows, or does it siphon away resources without offering substantial returns?

The same principle applies to experiences. A vacation might initially seem like a liability because it costs money upfront. But if it provides rejuvenation, meaningful memories, and helps you return to your daily responsibilities with renewed focus, it could be considered an asset for your mental well-being and productivity. The nuance in assessing assets versus liabilities lies in understanding the broader context of your goals and financial picture.

Building a financial portfolio full of assets while minimizing liabilities requires deliberate and consistent effort. Start by auditing your current financial commitments. List every expense and categorize them as either an asset or liability. Be honest about their real impact on your financial health. For liabilities, devise a plan to reduce or eliminate them over time. For assets, strategize ways to nurture and grow their value. Remember, it's not about being overly frugal or sacrificing every enjoyment; it's about ensuring that the majority of your decisions contribute positively to your long-term financial security and freedom.

Building a financial portfolio full of assets while minimizing liabilities requires effort and intentionality. Start by identifying the liabilities in your financial life. Do you have credit card debt from unnecessary purchases? Are you holding onto a subscription or membership you no longer use? These are the financial red flags to swipe left on. Once you've identified them, work on phasing them out. Pay down debt, cancel unused subscriptions, and think twice before making impulsive purchases. The process of eliminating liabilities might feel like cleaning up after a string of bad dates, but the relief and clarity it brings are worth it.

On the other hand, prioritize swiping right on assets. These are the investments and choices that align with your long-term goals. Contributing to a retirement fund, building an emergency savings account, or investing in professional development are all ways to strengthen your financial foundation. Each time you choose an asset over a liability, you're swiping right on your future self. It's like finding the perfect match who makes you feel secure, supported, and motivated to grow.

Think of it as curating a financial relationship profile. You want your portfolio to reflect stability, growth, and security. This doesn't mean you can't enjoy life or indulge occasionally. The key is to ensure your indulgences don't come at the expense of your financial health. Like in dating, balance is everything. A life full of only work and no play isn't sustainable—but neither is one full of financial red flags. The occasional indulgence, like a splurge on a memorable experience or a treat for yourself, is perfectly fine if it fits within your overall goals.

Spotting financial keepers and avoiding liabilities requires a mindset shift. It's about moving away from instant gratification and focusing on the bigger picture. When faced with a decision, consider how it fits into your long-term financial goals. Does this bring you closer to financial independence, or is it a temporary thrill that could set you back? The ability to discern between short-term satisfaction and long-term value is like having the ultimate relationship radar—one that keeps you on track for success.

Remember, every decision you make is a swipe that affects your financial journey. With the right mindset and a commitment to choosing wisely, you can build a financial life full of assets and ditch the liabilities for good. Just like finding the right partner in life, the right financial choices will bring you stability, growth, and a sense of fulfillment that lasts far beyond the initial thrill. So keep swiping wisely—your financial soulmate is out there.

Money Myths: Lies You've Been Spending On

The world of personal finance is riddled with myths—half-truths and misconceptions that often steer us down the wrong path. These myths are perpetuated by well-meaning friends, family, and even the media. They sound reasonable on the surface, but following them can lead to missed opportunities, poor financial decisions, and a sense of frustration when you can't seem to get ahead. Many of these myths stem from outdated beliefs or oversimplified advice that doesn't account for the complexities of modern financial systems. They can create mental blocks that prevent people from taking proactive steps toward financial stability and wealth-building.

Let's start by acknowledging that everyone's financial journey is unique, and blanket advice often fails to address individual circumstances. This makes it even more crucial to separate fact from fiction. For example, the belief that "renting is throwing money away" might work for someone who's ready to settle down and buy a home, but it could be disastrous advice for someone who needs the flexibility of renting to pursue career opportunities in different cities. Similarly, the myth that you need a six-figure income to invest often stops people from taking small but significant steps toward their financial future.

Addressing these myths requires not just debunking them but replacing them with actionable truths that empower individuals to make informed choices. By doing so, you can pave the way for smarter financial decisions that align with your goals and values. The key is to question conventional wisdom, seek reliable information, and remain adaptable as your financial circumstances evolve. Let's debunk some of the most persistent money myths and uncover strategies that will truly empower you to take control of your financial future.

Myth #1: You need a six-figure income to save or invest.

One of the most damaging misconceptions is that saving and investing are only for the wealthy. Many people believe that they need a large income to start building wealth, but this couldn't be further from the truth. The key to financial success isn't how much you earn—it's how you manage what you earn. Even small, consistent contributions to a savings account or investment portfolio can grow significantly over time thanks to the power of compound interest. For example, investing just £50 a month in a low-cost index fund with a 7% annual return can grow to over £12,000 in 10 years. The secret lies in starting early and staying consistent, regardless of your income level.

Myth #2: Debt is a necessary part of life.

Debt has been normalized to the point where many people believe it's unavoidable. Whether it's student loans, car payments, or credit card balances, society often treats debt as a rite of passage. While certain types of debt, like a mortgage or student loans for a high-earning profession, can be considered strategic, not all debt is created equal. High-interest consumer debt, such as credit cards or payday loans, is a financial trap that can derail your progress. Breaking free from the "debt is necessary" mindset starts with recognizing that living within your means and prioritizing saving over borrowing are the real keys to financial freedom.

Myth #3: Renting is throwing money away.

"Why rent when you can buy?" is a common refrain, but the idea that renting is inherently wasteful is a myth. Owning a home comes with significant upfront costs, like a down payment, closing fees, and maintenance expenses. Renting, on the other hand, provides flexibility and often includes fewer financial responsibilities. If you're not ready to commit to a location or don't have the financial stability to handle the hidden costs of homeownership, renting can be a smart and practical choice. The real "waste" isn't in renting—it's in stretching your finances to the breaking point to buy a home you're not prepared to afford.

Myth #4: Budgeting means giving up all the fun.

The word "budget" often conjures images of sacrifice and deprivation. Many people believe that sticking to a budget means cutting out everything enjoyable, like dining out or traveling. In reality, a good budget isn't about eliminating fun; it's about prioritizing it. A well-crafted budget allows you to spend on the things that truly matter to you while ensuring your essential needs and savings goals are covered. By aligning your spending with your values, you can enjoy life's pleasures without guilt or financial strain.

Myth #5: You can always make up for lost time later.

It's tempting to think that you can delay saving or investing and catch up later. This mindset often leads to procrastination, which can be costly. The longer you wait to start saving, the more you miss out on the benefits of compound growth. For instance, if you start saving £200 a month at age 25, you could have over £220,000 by age 65 with a 7% annual return. If you wait until age 35 to start, you'd have to save almost double that amount monthly to achieve the same result. Time is your most valuable ally in building wealth, so the best time to start is now.

Myth #6: Buying in bulk always saves money.

The allure of bulk shopping is strong, with the promise of lower prices per unit. However, buying in bulk isn't always the money-saving strategy it's made out to be. If you end up wasting perishable items or buying things you don't actually need, the savings disappear. Bulk buying makes sense for non-perishables or items you use frequently, but it's essential to evaluate whether the larger quantities align with your actual consumption patterns. Sometimes, smaller, strategic purchases are the more economical choice.

Myth #7: You should always prioritize paying off debt over investing.

While paying off debt is important, focusing exclusively on debt repayment at the expense of investing can be a mistake. The key is to strike a balance. If your debt has a low interest rate—say, under 5%—it may make sense to invest simultaneously, as the returns on your investments could outpace the cost of the debt. For example, if you're paying off a student loan with a 3% interest rate, but your investments are earning 7% annually, you're building wealth faster by doing both. High-interest debt, however, should take priority, as it's more difficult to overcome.

Myth #8: More income automatically means more wealth.

Earning more money doesn't guarantee financial security. Lifestyle inflation—the tendency to spend more as your income increases—can erode any extra earnings. It's not uncommon for high earners to live paycheck to paycheck because their spending keeps pace with their income. True wealth is built by managing your money wisely, not just by earning more of it. Living below your means and investing the difference is the formula for long-term financial success.

Myth #9: You need to know everything about investing before you start.

Many people delay investing because they feel they don't know enough or fear making mistakes. The truth is, you don't need to be an expert to begin. Start with simple, low-cost options like index funds, which offer broad market exposure and require minimal management. The most important step is getting started. You can learn and adjust your strategy as you go, but waiting until you feel completely confident could cost you valuable time in the market.

Myth #10: Financial success is about luck.

It's easy to look at wealthy individuals and assume they got lucky—inherited money, won the lottery, or stumbled into a lucrative opportunity. While luck can play a role, financial success is overwhelmingly about discipline, planning, and perseverance. Building wealth requires setting clear goals, creating a plan, and sticking to it, even when it's challenging. Luck might open a door, but it's your actions that determine whether you walk through it and thrive.

By challenging these myths and embracing a more informed approach to money, you can avoid common pitfalls and set yourself up for long-term success. Personal finance isn't about following one-size-fits-all rules; it's about making thoughtful choices that align with your goals and values. With the right mindset and a commitment to breaking free from these myths, you can take control of your financial future and thrive.

Part 2: Building a Strong Financial Foundation

Budget Like a Boss (Without Crying)

Budgeting is often misunderstood. People think it's all about sacrifice and restriction, but at its core, a budget is about freedom. It's the freedom to spend without guilt, save without hesitation, and plan without stress. When you budget effectively, you're telling your money where to go, rather than wondering where it went. This chapter is all about transforming budgeting into a tool you love to use, rather than a dreaded task.

The first step to budgeting like a boss is getting clear on your financial picture. Start by tracking your income and expenses. For one month, jot down every pound you earn and spend. Apps like YNAB (You Need A Budget) or Mint can make this easier, or you can go old-school with a notebook. The goal here is awareness, not judgment. Once you have a clear view, categorize your expenses into fixed (rent, utilities), variable (groceries, transport), and discretionary (entertainment, dining out). This gives you the framework to craft a budget tailored to your life.

Next, set goals that excite you and truly resonate with your values. What do you want your money to do for you? Maybe it's paying off debt, building an emergency fund, saving for a dream holiday, or investing in your future. Goals should be specific, measurable, and tied to your life aspirations—-the things that light a fire in you and keep you motivated, even when the road gets tough. Whether it's something small like saving for a weekend getaway or a life-changing milestone like buying a home, your goals provide purpose and direction. Writing these goals down transforms your budget from a rigid list of numbers into a living, breathing strategy for creating the life you envision.

Think of these goals as your personal mission statement for money. What truly matters to you? Is it financial security, freedom to travel, or the ability to give back to causes you care about? When you set goals that align with your core values, budgeting stops feeling like a chore and starts feeling like an empowering process. It's about working toward something meaningful, not just tracking numbers. For example, if family is your top priority, saving for a family holiday or contributing to a child's education fund might take precedence. On the other hand, if independence and exploration drive you, you might prioritize building a travel fund or investing in personal development.

Once your goals are clear, break them down into actionable steps. If your dream is to save £5,000 for a down payment on a car, divide that goal into smaller monthly targets based on your timeline. Breaking big goals into manageable chunks makes them feel more achievable and helps you stay motivated as you hit each milestone. Celebrate your progress along the way—each small win builds momentum and reinforces your commitment to the bigger picture. By doing this, your goals evolve from abstract ideas into tangible, attainable outcomes.

Now, let's tackle the common budgeting complaint: it's too rigid. Life is unpredictable, and your budget should reflect that. Build flexibility into your plan by creating a buffer category for unexpected expenses. This way, when your car needs a repair or your friend's birthday pops up, you can handle it without derailing your progress. Think of this buffer as your "just-in-case" safety valve, a cushion that allows your budget to breathe while keeping you aligned with your larger financial objectives. Planning for the unpredictable gives you peace of mind and keeps your budget sustainable.

One trick to staying consistent is making budgeting fun and personal. Turn it into a monthly ritual with your favorite snacks, music, or even a cozy setup where you can feel at ease while reviewing your finances. Use tools like visual progress trackers, goal charts, or apps to make the process interactive and engaging. Celebrate small wins, like meeting a savings milestone or successfully reducing an unnecessary expense. Positive reinforcement—even if it's just treating yourself to a small indulgence—helps keep you motivated and reminds you that budgeting isn't about punishment; it's about empowerment and freedom.

Finally, make reviewing your budget a regular habit. Financial success isn't static—your income, goals, and priorities will evolve over time, and your budget should, too. Dedicate time at the end of each month to evaluate your progress and reflect on your achievements. Celebrate what went well and take note of any challenges or areas where you might have overspent. By analyzing these patterns, you can identify opportunities for improvement and set more realistic targets for the next month. This isn't about perfection—it's about progress and understanding how your habits align with your larger goals.

This monthly review process transforms budgeting from a rigid chore into a dynamic and evolving tool. Use this time to refine your approach. For instance, if you notice that certain categories consistently exceed their budget, consider adjusting your allocations or finding creative ways to reduce those expenses. Perhaps your dining-out costs are higher than planned; this might be an opportunity to explore meal prepping or set limits on how often you treat yourself. Conversely, if you're consistently underspending in a particular area, you could redirect those funds toward savings or a goal that excites you.

Don't be afraid to experiment with different budgeting styles until you find the one that works best for you. From zero-based budgeting, where every pound is allocated a purpose, to the 50/30/20 rule, which divides your income into needs, wants, and savings, there are plenty of approaches to try. As your financial situation changes—perhaps through a new job, a side hustle, or unexpected expenses—your budget should remain flexible and adaptable.

Another benefit of regular reviews is the opportunity to reassess your financial goals. As you make progress, you might find that your priorities shift. Perhaps paying off debt was your initial focus, but now you're ready to start building an investment portfolio. Or maybe an emergency fund that once seemed out of reach is now fully funded, allowing you to focus on longer-term aspirations like travel or homeownership. These check-ins keep your goals fresh and relevant, motivating you to stay engaged with your budget.

Remember, budgeting is a journey, not a destination. It's a skill that improves with practice and becomes second nature over time. Each adjustment you make brings you closer to financial freedom and peace of mind—a priceless gift to your present and future self.

Budgeting doesn't have to be scary or overwhelming. It's a skill that improves with practice and becomes second nature over time. With the right mindset and tools, you can take charge of your finances, turn your goals into realities, and build a foundation for lasting success. Each decision you make to stay within your budget is a step toward greater financial freedom and peace of mind—a gift to your present and future self.

Emergency Funds: The Financial First-Aid Kit

Life has a way of throwing curveballs when you least expect them. Whether it's a sudden car repair, an unexpected medical bill, or a surprise expense that pops up out of nowhere, these moments can wreak havoc on your finances if you're not prepared. That's where an emergency fund comes in—your financial first-aid kit, ready to protect you when life's uncertainties strike. An emergency fund is not just a safety net; it's a powerful tool that can help you navigate life's challenges with confidence and peace of mind.

An emergency fund serves as a financial buffer, allowing you to handle unexpected expenses without relying on credit cards, loans, or dipping into your long-term savings. It's the difference between a minor inconvenience and a major financial setback. Imagine the relief of knowing that if your car breaks down, you can cover the cost without worrying about how it will affect your rent or grocery budget. That's the security an emergency fund provides.

Building an emergency fund might sound intimidating, especially if you're already working with a tight budget. But the key is to start small and stay consistent. Begin by setting a realistic goal. Financial experts often recommend having three to six months' worth of living expenses saved, but don't let that number overwhelm you. Start with a smaller milestone, like £500 or £1,000. This initial amount is enough to cover most minor emergencies and gives you a sense of accomplishment as you work toward a larger goal. Every small step forward builds confidence and demonstrates that creating a financial safety net is achievable.

To help guide you through this process, let's break it down into actionable targets for building your emergency fund:

1. **Three-Month Fund:** Calculate your essential monthly expenses, such as rent or mortgage payments, utilities, groceries, and transportation. Multiply this total by three to find your target for a three-month fund. For instance, if your monthly essentials total £2,000, your three-month emergency fund goal would be £6,000. This provides a solid safety net for shorter disruptions like a temporary layoff or medical leave.
2. **Six-Month Fund:** To increase your financial resilience, aim for six months' worth of essential expenses. Using the same

example of £2,000 per month, your six-month goal would be £12,000. This is especially valuable if you work in a volatile industry or want to plan for more extended periods of uncertainty, such as a major career transition.
3. **Twelve-Month Fund:** For ultimate peace of mind, consider saving for a full year's worth of essential expenses. While ambitious, this £24,000 goal (using the same £2,000 monthly expense example) offers unparalleled financial security. It's ideal for those who want maximum flexibility, such as entrepreneurs building a business or individuals nearing retirement who want extra security.

Breaking these goals into smaller steps and focusing on one milestone at a time makes the process less overwhelming. Celebrate your achievements along the way, whether it's reaching the first £500 or hitting a significant benchmark like a three-month cushion. Each milestone reinforces your progress and builds momentum toward larger financial goals.

Automating your savings is one of the easiest ways to build your emergency fund. Set up a direct deposit or automatic transfer from your paycheck into a dedicated savings account. By doing this, you remove the temptation to spend that money and ensure that your emergency fund grows consistently. Treat your savings like any other fixed expense—just as you would pay your rent or utility bills, make saving for your emergency fund a non-negotiable priority.

Choosing the right place to store your emergency fund is also important. A high-yield savings account is often a great option, as it allows your money to earn interest while remaining easily accessible. The key is to keep your emergency fund separate from your regular checking or savings account to avoid accidentally dipping into it for nonemergencies. This separation reinforces the purpose of the fund and helps you maintain discipline.

Building an emergency fund also requires a shift in mindset. Think of it as your personal insurance policy against life's unpredictability. Instead of viewing it as money you can't touch, see it as a tool that empowers you to handle challenges without derailing your financial progress. This perspective makes the process of saving feel less like a sacrifice and more like an investment in your own stability and well-being.

If you're struggling to find extra money to save, start by looking for small, manageable changes in your spending habits. Can you cut back on dining out or skip a few impulse purchases? Even saving just £20 a week adds up over time. Side hustles or selling unused items can also provide a quick boost to your fund. Remember, the goal is progress, not perfection. Every pound you save brings you closer to the security and peace of mind that an emergency fund offers.

Once you've reached your initial goal, keep the momentum going. Aim to build a larger fund that can cover three to six months' worth of essential expenses, such as housing, utilities, groceries, and transportation. This larger cushion provides a safety net in case of more significant disruptions, like a job loss or major medical issue. Reaching this level of financial preparedness might take time, but the sense of security it provides is invaluable.

It's also important to know when to use your emergency fund. Reserve it for true emergencies—situations that are urgent, necessary, and unexpected. A flash sale on a new TV or a spontaneous weekend getaway doesn't qualify. However, unexpected medical expenses, car repairs, or temporary income loss do. Using your emergency fund wisely ensures that it remains intact for when you truly need it.

Replenishing your emergency fund after using it is just as crucial as building it in the first place. Treat it like any other financial goal by redirecting savings or allocating part of your budget to rebuild the fund. The faster you can restore it, the better prepared you'll be for the next unexpected event. To make it even easier to protect and rebuild your fund, consider placing it in a locked or high-yield savings account. These accounts make it slightly harder to access the money on impulse, ensuring that it's reserved exclusively for true emergencies.

The key to maintaining a robust emergency fund is discipline. Avoid dipping into it for non-urgent or avoidable expenses. It's tempting to use the fund for things like a great deal on a vacation or upgrading your gadgets, but this defeats its purpose. By viewing your emergency fund as untouchable except in genuine emergencies, you reinforce its role as a financial lifeline. Having the money in a separate account—or even a fixed-term account where withdrawals require extra steps—adds an additional layer of protection, reducing the likelihood of accidental or impulsive spending.

Replenishing your fund after you've used it should be a top priority. Treat it as part of your recovery plan after an unexpected expense, just like you would rebuild a bridge after it's been crossed in a storm. Allocate a portion of your income to restoring the fund each month, and if possible, use windfalls like bonuses, tax refunds, or side hustle earnings to speed up the process. A fully replenished emergency fund isn't just a financial safety net; it's a powerful symbol of your resilience and preparedness for whatever life may bring.

An emergency fund isn't just about money; it's about peace of mind and empowerment. It's about knowing that when life inevitably throws challenges your way—be it an unexpected car repair, a sudden medical bill, or even a temporary loss of income—you're prepared. This sense of readiness allows you to approach these situations with resilience and focus, rather than panic and stress. Imagine the confidence that comes from knowing you can weather financial storms without relying on credit cards, loans, or dipping into your long-term savings. That's the true power of an emergency fund.

By prioritizing your emergency fund, you're not just preparing for the unexpected—you're actively taking control of your financial narrative. It's a statement of independence and self-reliance, a declaration that you won't let unforeseen events derail your progress. Beyond the practical benefits, it fosters a profound sense of security and well-being, freeing you to focus on your broader goals without the constant shadow of "what if" looming over your head. Building and maintaining this fund is more than a financial strategy—it's an investment in your peace of mind and a cornerstone of true financial freedom.

The Debt Detox: Breaking Up with Bad Habits

Debt can feel like a toxic relationship. It drains your energy, keeps you stuck in a cycle of anxiety, and prevents you from focusing on the things that truly matter. But just like any unhealthy relationship, breaking up with bad financial habits is possible—and necessary for your long-term well-being. This section is all about detoxing from debt and building a healthier, more secure financial future.

The first step in any debt detox is acknowledgment. It's crucial to take a clear, honest look at your financial situation. Start by making a comprehensive list of all your debts. This includes noting the creditor's name, the total amount owed, the interest rate, and the minimum monthly payment for each debt. Organize this list from the highest interest rate to the lowest, as this will give you a clear picture of which debts are costing you the most and where to focus your repayment efforts.

Creating this list might be uncomfortable, especially if the numbers feel overwhelming, but confronting the reality of your financial situation is a necessary first step. Debt can feel like an abstract, insurmountable problem when it's swirling in your mind. Turning it into concrete, manageable data allows you to take control and start strategizing. Seeing everything laid out in front of you transforms the problem from an emotional weight into a solvable equation. It's the foundation of an effective debt repayment plan and empowers you to move forward with clarity and purpose.

Once you have a clear picture of your debts, prioritize them based on a structured repayment strategy. Two popular methods for tackling debt are:

- **The Snowball Method**: This approach focuses on paying off your smallest debts first while making minimum payments on all others. The idea is to build momentum by achieving quick wins, which can boost your confidence and motivation. For example, if you have three debts—£500, £2,000, and £4,000—you would pay off the £500 debt first. Once cleared, the money you were putting toward it is rolled into the next smallest debt, creating a snowball effect. This method prioritizes psychological benefits, making it ideal for individuals who need encouragement to stick with their plan.
- **The Avalanche Method**: This method targets debts with the highest interest rates first, regardless of their balances. By focusing on high-interest debts, you minimize the total amount paid over time. For instance, if you have debts of £1,000 at 8% interest, £2,000 at 20% interest, and £4,000 at 15% interest, you would prioritize the £2,000 debt first. While it might take longer to see your first debt eliminated, the avalanche method saves more money in the long run, making it ideal for those who are motivated by financial efficiency.

Choosing between these methods depends on your goals and what motivates you. If seeing immediate progress keeps you committed, the snowball method may be best. If saving money is your priority, the avalanche method could be more effective. Whichever you choose, the most important thing is consistency. Stick to your plan, and over time, you'll see tangible results that reinforce your efforts.

Budgeting plays a critical role in your debt detox. A well-structured budget ensures that you're dedicating enough of your income toward debt repayment while still covering your essential expenses. Start by taking a detailed look at your current spending habits and categorizing your expenses into fixed costs (like rent and utilities), variable costs (like groceries and transportation), and discretionary spending (like dining out or entertainment). This exercise will help you identify areas where you can cut back or redirect funds to accelerate debt repayment.

For example, consider skipping the daily coffee run occasionally rather than eliminating it entirely. Skipping your favorite latte once or twice a week won't make you rich, but it can free up a little extra money to put toward your financial goals. The idea isn't to completely remove life's pleasures, as that can lead to frustration and burnout. Instead, focus on moderation. For instance, prepare meals at home more often, but still allow yourself the occasional dining-out experience as a treat. Similarly, review your subscriptions to see which ones you truly value and cancel the ones that no longer serve you. Even these small changes can add up over time.

Redirect the savings you make from these adjustments directly toward your debt payments. For instance, if skipping two coffees a week saves you £15 and cooking at home instead of eating out saves another £40, you could redirect that £55 a month toward debt repayment. Apply it to the smallest debt in your snowball method or the highest-interest debt in your avalanche method. These additional payments may seem minor at first, but they create momentum and can significantly shorten your debt repayment timeline. By finding a balance between enjoying life's little pleasures and making conscious financial choices, you set yourself up for long-term success while maintaining a sense of satisfaction and control.

Additionally, consider creating a separate category in your budget specifically for extra debt payments. Label it as "debt acceleration fund" to give it a clear purpose and allocate any extra income—such as bonuses, tax refunds, or side hustle earnings—directly into this category. This ensures that every pound you save or earn is working toward freeing you from debt. Remember, small sacrifices now can lead to greater financial freedom and peace of mind in the future.

Another essential step is to stop accumulating new debt. This might mean putting your credit cards on ice—literally. Some people find it helpful to physically freeze their cards in a block of ice to make impulsive spending impossible. Others opt to delete saved credit card details from online shopping accounts. Whatever strategy works for you, the goal is to break the cycle of relying on debt for everyday expenses.

Consolidation can also be a useful tool in your debt detox journey. If you have multiple high-interest debts, consider consolidating them into a single loan with a lower interest rate. This simplifies your payments and can save you money over time. However, it's important to do your research and ensure that consolidation aligns with your financial goals.

As you work on paying off your debt, don't forget to celebrate your progress. Each debt paid off is a victory, no matter how small. These milestones are proof that you're moving in the right direction and building a healthier financial future. Reward yourself in meaningful, budget-friendly ways, like treating yourself to a favorite meal or enjoying a day out with loved ones. Celebrating your wins keeps you motivated and reinforces positive habits.

Equally important is addressing the habits and mindsets that led to debt in the first place. Reflect on your spending patterns and identify triggers for overspending. Are you prone to retail therapy when stressed? Do you find it hard to resist sales or discounts? Understanding these tendencies allows you to create strategies for avoiding debt traps in the future. For example, setting clear spending limits, using cash instead of credit, or implementing a 24-hour rule before making non-essential purchases can help you stay on track.

Finally, remind yourself that breaking free from debt is a journey, not a quick fix. It requires patience, persistence, and a willingness to learn from past mistakes. But with each step you take, you're reclaiming control over your finances and your life. The freedom and peace of mind that come from being debt-free are worth every ounce of effort. Remember, this is your financial detox—a clean break from the habits and patterns that held you back, and a fresh start toward a brighter, more secure future.

Maximizing Your Pension: Planting the Seeds for Retirement

Why Pensions (UK) Are Crucial for Long-Term Wealth

Pensions are one of the most powerful tools for securing financial stability in retirement, yet they're often overlooked or misunderstood. In the UK, pensions provide tax advantages that accelerate the growth of your savings and often include employer contributions that boost your pot even further. This makes them an essential component of long-term wealth-building.

The tax benefits of pensions are significant, making them one of the most efficient ways to save for retirement. When you contribute to a pension, you receive tax relief from the government, which acts as an immediate boost to your contributions. For basic-rate taxpayers, this means that for every £80 you contribute, the government adds an extra £20, effectively increasing your savings by 25%. Higher-rate taxpayers benefit even more, as they can claim additional relief through their tax return, turning a £80 contribution into £133.33 in their pension pot. Over time, this advantage compounds, significantly amplifying the growth of your retirement savings.

The power of compounding cannot be overstated. By reinvesting the returns from your contributions, your savings grow exponentially over the years. For example, a single contribution of £1,000 at age 30 could grow to nearly £4,000 by age 65, assuming a 6% annual return. Multiply this by consistent monthly contributions and the impact becomes monumental. This combination of tax relief and compounding makes pensions an unparalleled tool for building long-term wealth.

Furthermore, pensions provide a level of discipline in saving. Since the funds are typically inaccessible until retirement age, they ensure that your savings remain untouched and continue to grow. This built-in restriction helps prevent impulsive withdrawals that could derail your long-term plans. Combined with employer contributions and the ability to invest in a range of assets, pensions offer a structured and highly beneficial way to secure your financial future.

Moreover, many employers offer workplace pensions with contributions that match or exceed what you put in, up to a certain percentage of your salary. This is essentially free money, and failing to take full advantage of it is like leaving part of your paycheck unclaimed. Combined with tax relief, employer contributions can double or even triple the amount you're saving for retirement, giving your pension a significant head start.

How to Consolidate Pensions from Previous Jobs into One Manageable Plan

Throughout your career, you may accumulate several pensions from different employers. Keeping track of these scattered pots can be challenging, and failing to manage them properly can lead to inefficiencies and missed opportunities for growth. Consolidating these pensions into one manageable plan simplifies your finances and ensures your retirement savings are working as hard as possible.

To begin, locate all your pensions. In the UK, the Pension Tracing Service can help you find plans from previous employers. Once you've gathered the details—including balances, fees, and investment performance—you can evaluate your options for consolidation.

One popular choice is transferring your pensions into a Self-Invested Personal Pension (SIPP). SIPPs provide more control over how your money is invested, offering a wider range of options compared to traditional workplace pensions. Alternatively, you might consolidate your pensions under your current employer's plan, provided it offers competitive fees and investment choices.

When consolidating, it is important to thoroughly assess any potential exit fees or unique benefits tied to your existing pensions. Some older pension plans may offer valuable features, such as guaranteed annuities, enhanced tax-free lump sums, or higher interest rates, which could be forfeited upon transfer. These perks can significantly impact your retirement income, making it critical to carefully evaluate whether the benefits of consolidation outweigh the potential losses. Additionally, consider how consolidation might affect your overall investment strategy and the flexibility of accessing funds in the future.

Consulting with a qualified financial advisor can be invaluable during this process. They can provide personalized advice on the pros and cons of consolidation, help identify hidden costs, and ensure that the decision aligns with your long-term retirement goals. Taking the time to fully understand the implications of transferring pensions can prevent costly mistakes and help you make the most of your retirement savings.

Ensure You're Not Leaving Free Money on the Table

One of the simplest ways to maximize your pension is to ensure you're taking full advantage of employer contributions. Many employers match your contributions up to a specific percentage of your salary—often around 5%. For instance, if you earn £30,000 annually and contribute 5% (£1,500), your employer will add an additional £1,500. That's an immediate 100% return on your investment, even before factoring in tax relief or investment growth.

To ensure you're not leaving money on the table:

1. **Contribute Enough to Get the Full Match**: Check your employer's policy and contribute at least the minimum required to receive the full match. This is free money you don't want to miss out on. By contributing enough to meet the full match, you maximize your retirement savings without significantly altering your budget, as the employer's contribution effectively doubles your investment. Think of it as an instant return on your money—for every pound you contribute, you're essentially getting an additional pound added to your pension pot by your employer. Over time, this matching contribution not only grows with investment returns but also significantly accelerates the size of your overall retirement savings. If you're

unsure about your employer's contribution policy, take the time to review your benefits or speak with your HR department. Understanding this benefit fully ensures you're not leaving any money on the table, and it allows you to optimize your contributions in a way that maximizes your financial advantage over the long term.

2. **Review Your Contributions Regularly**: As your salary increases, adjust your pension contributions to maintain the same percentage or even increase it. For example, if you receive a raise, consider directing a portion of that increase directly into your pension. This approach allows your savings to grow in proportion to your earnings and ensures you are consistently building towards a secure retirement. Many people set their contribution rate when they start a job and forget to update it, missing out on opportunities to save more as their financial situation improves.

Regularly reviewing your contributions—at least annually—ensures that your pension plan remains aligned with your current salary and financial goals. Take this opportunity to check if you're taking full advantage of any employer matching contributions. If your employer increases their matching percentage or adjusts their pension policy, you want to make sure you're optimizing your benefits.

Additionally, reassessing your contributions can help you identify other areas for improvement. For instance, if your living expenses have decreased—perhaps due to paying off a loan or lowering your monthly bills—redirecting those funds into your pension can accelerate your progress. Over time, small incremental increases in your contributions can have a substantial impact, thanks to the compounding growth of your investments.

By staying proactive and revisiting your contributions regularly, you ensure you're not falling behind on your retirement goals while maximizing the potential of every salary increase. It's a habit that can transform your financial future and give you greater peace of mind as you plan for the years ahead.

> 3. **Automate Increases**: If your employer allows it, set up automatic contribution increases. For example, you can increase your contributions by 1% annually or whenever you receive a raise. Automating these increases makes the process effortless and ensures your pension contributions grow alongside your income. By embedding these adjustments into your financial routine, you take the guesswork out of consistently building your retirement fund.

Over time, these small, incremental increases can result in significant growth in your pension pot. For instance, an annual 1% increase in contributions may seem minor, but compounded over decades, it can add tens of thousands of pounds to your retirement savings. If you begin with a modest 5% contribution at age 30 and increase it by 1% each year until you reach 15%, you could accumulate significantly more wealth by retirement compared to maintaining a flat contribution rate.

Automating increases also helps you adjust to saving more without feeling the financial strain. When contributions grow incrementally, the changes are often subtle and easier to manage within your budget. For example, directing part of a raise or bonus toward your pension ensures that you continue living within your means while taking advantage of your increased income. This strategy prevents lifestyle inflation—the tendency to spend more as you earn more—and ensures that your financial priorities remain focused on long-term goals.

Additionally, many pension providers and employers offer tools to automate these increases, making it a straightforward process. Take advantage of these features to set your contributions on autopilot. Not only does this reduce the effort required to manually adjust your pension each year, but it also ensures you remain disciplined in your approach to saving for retirement. By taking action now, you lay the groundwork for a more substantial and secure pension pot, providing peace of mind as you approach your golden years.

4. **Understand Employer Vesting Schedules**: Some employers require you to stay with the company for a certain period before their contributions fully vest. For example, an employer might have a three-year vesting schedule, meaning you'll only own their contributions if you stay for three years. Be aware of these timelines, especially if you're considering changing jobs. Understanding vesting schedules can help you make informed decisions about job transitions and ensure you don't leave unvested contributions behind.

Understanding your pension fund

Understanding what your pension is being invested into is a crucial aspect of ensuring your retirement savings are working effectively for you. Many people contribute to their pension without fully knowing where their money is allocated or how it is performing. This lack of oversight can lead to suboptimal growth, unnecessary fees, or investments that don't align with your financial goals or risk tolerance.

Start by reviewing the investment options offered by your pension provider. Most pensions have a default fund where contributions are automatically allocated, often a mixed-asset fund with moderate risk. While these funds are designed to suit a broad range of savers, they may not align with your specific retirement timeline or financial ambitions. For example, if you're younger and have decades until retirement, you might benefit from a more aggressive investment strategy with a higher allocation to equities, which typically offer better long-term growth. Conversely, if you're closer to retirement, shifting toward bonds or lower-risk investments can help protect your savings from market volatility.

Analyzing your pension's performance is equally important. Look at the historical returns of your investments and compare them to similar funds or benchmarks. If your fund is underperforming or charging high fees, consider switching to a different option within your pension plan or even transferring to a provider with better investment choices and lower costs. Remember, even a small difference in fees or returns can significantly impact the size of your pension pot over time.

Additionally, consider how your investments align with your personal values or ethical preferences. Many pension providers now offer socially responsible or ESG (Environmental, Social, and Governance) funds that focus on sustainable and ethical investments. If this is important to you, explore these options and make adjustments as needed.

Finally, make it a habit to review your pension investments annually. Life circumstances and market conditions change, and your investment strategy should adapt accordingly. Whether it's reallocating funds, increasing contributions, or choosing a different risk profile, staying proactive about your pension investments ensures you're on track for a secure and comfortable retirement.

The Long-Term Impact of Maximizing Your Pension

Small steps taken today can lead to significant results over time. For example, contributing an additional £100 per month from age 30 to 65 could add over £100,000 to your pension pot, assuming a 6% annual return. The combination of tax relief, employer contributions, and compound interest makes pensions an unparalleled vehicle for retirement savings.

Moreover, the earlier you start maximizing your pension contributions, the more time you give your investments to grow and benefit from the incredible power of compound interest. Compound interest works best when it has decades to build upon itself, turning modest contributions into substantial wealth over time. For instance, contributing just £100 per month starting at age 25 could grow to over £200,000 by age 65, assuming a 6% annual return. This exponential growth happens because you're not just earning returns on your initial contributions but also on the returns those contributions generate year after year.

Even if you're starting later in life, it's never too late to make meaningful strides toward building your pension pot. Increasing your contributions now—even by small amounts—can still lead to significant improvements in your retirement savings. For example, a £200 monthly increase in contributions at age 40 could grow to over £100,000 by age 65, depending on your investment performance. The key is consistency and staying committed to maximizing your savings wherever possible.

The beauty of starting early or making consistent contributions later is that it gives you greater flexibility and peace of mind. Early savers often have the advantage of being able to reduce their contributions slightly later in life if necessary, without jeopardizing their long-term goals. Meanwhile, those starting late can offset the shorter timeframe by taking advantage of employer contributions, tax relief, and more aggressive investment strategies to catch up. Every effort you make now sets the stage for a more secure and comfortable retirement.

By consolidating old pensions, maximizing employer contributions, and staying proactive about your savings, you're setting yourself up for a secure and fulfilling retirement. Start now, and your future self will thank you.

Part 3: Growing Wealth for the Future

Investing: Let's Make Money Make Money

Investing is one of the most transformative ways to grow wealth and achieve financial independence. Unlike saving, which keeps your money idle, investing gives it a purpose—a way to multiply over time. While the concept of investing might seem intimidating, particularly with the risks and unfamiliar terms often associated with it, it's far more accessible than many realize. With a foundational understanding and a disciplined approach, anyone can begin building wealth and creating a more secure financial future.

Why Investing Matters

Money sitting in a savings account may feel safe, but it's losing value every year due to inflation. Inflation steadily erodes the purchasing power of money, meaning that what £100 buys today may cost significantly more in the future. Investing provides a counterbalance to this erosion by offering the potential for growth that outpaces inflation. By choosing to invest, you're not only preserving your money's value but actively growing it. This growth creates opportunities—whether it's for a comfortable retirement, buying a home, funding education, or leaving a legacy.

Investing bridges the gap between simply saving and building true wealth. It transforms your money from a passive resource into an active participant in your financial journey. The concept is simple: make your money work harder than you do. For example, a savings account might offer 1% annual interest, barely keeping pace with inflation, while a diversified investment portfolio could average returns of 6-8% over time. Though this difference may seem small at first glance, it grows exponentially over decades thanks to the magic of compounding. Compounding ensures that not only do your initial investments generate returns, but those returns themselves begin to grow and multiply over time. This snowball effect accelerates your wealth-building, turning modest contributions into substantial assets.

For instance, investing £10,000 at a 7% annual return would grow to nearly £20,000 in 10 years. Over 30 years, that same initial amount could grow to almost £80,000 without any additional contributions. Now imagine adding consistent monthly contributions to the equation—the results become even more dramatic. This is the true power of investing: a disciplined and patient approach allows you to reap the benefits of long-term growth while inflation and time work in your favor instead of against you. By leveraging this strategy, you're not just preserving your money's value; you're actively working to multiply it, creating opportunities for financial freedom and a secure future.

The Basics of Investing

Before diving into the world of investing, it's essential to understand some foundational principles. These aren't just academic concepts; they're practical tools that guide every investment decision.

- **Risk vs. Reward**: Every investment carries a degree of risk. Generally, higher potential rewards are associated with higher risks. For instance, stocks have historically provided strong returns over time but can be highly volatile in the short term. Conversely, bonds are more stable but offer lower returns. Understanding your comfort level with risk is crucial when deciding where to invest your money.
- **Diversification**: The age-old adage "Don't put all your eggs in one basket" perfectly encapsulates this concept. Diversification involves spreading your investments across various assets,

industries, and regions. By doing so, you reduce the impact of a poor-performing investment. For example, if one stock in your portfolio performs poorly but others perform well, your overall losses are mitigated.

- **Compound Growth**: Time is your best friend when it comes to investing. Compound growth occurs when your returns generate their own returns. Even modest, consistent contributions grow substantially over decades. For example, investing £100 a month at an average annual return of 7% can grow to nearly £120,000 over 30 years.
- **Time Horizon**: Your investment strategy should align with your financial goals and the time you have to achieve them. If your goal is decades away, you can afford to take on more risk. However, for short-term goals, safer investments are often more appropriate to preserve capital.

Types of Investments

There are various types of assets to invest in, each with its own risk-reward profile. Understanding these will help you build a well-rounded portfolio:

- **Stocks**: Representing ownership in a company, stocks are a cornerstone of wealth creation. They offer high growth potential but are subject to market volatility. Investing in individual companies requires research and an understanding of market trends. When you buy a stock, you are purchasing a share of a company's future profits and growth. This can be incredibly rewarding over time, as businesses expand, innovate, and generate higher revenues.

Stocks are often divided into categories such as growth stocks, which focus on companies expected to grow at an above-average rate, and dividend stocks, which provide regular income to shareholders through dividends. Growth stocks may not pay dividends but reinvest their earnings to fuel further expansion. This makes them attractive to long-term investors who are seeking higher capital appreciation.

However, with high potential rewards comes higher risk. Stock prices can fluctuate wildly due to market conditions, company performance, and external economic factors. This volatility means that while you might see rapid gains, there's also the potential for significant losses in the short term. Successful stock investing requires a balance between understanding individual companies and diversifying to mitigate risks. Many investors also use index funds or ETFs to invest in stocks collectively, reducing the need for extensive research while capturing the overall market's performance.

For beginners, starting with stocks of well-established companies, often referred to as blue-chip stocks, can provide a stable introduction to the market. These companies typically have strong track records, reliable dividends, and a level of resilience during market downturns. Investing in stocks is a journey that rewards patience, research, and a long-term perspective.

- **Bonds**: Bonds are essentially loans made to governments or corporations in exchange for interest payments. They're less volatile than stocks and are often used to provide stability within a portfolio. For example, government bonds, often referred to as gilts in the UK, are seen as safe investments, while corporate bonds may offer higher returns but carry more risk. Bonds are often used by investors looking to diversify and reduce the overall risk in their portfolio.
- **Real Estate**: Investing in property can generate rental income and capital appreciation. While it requires significant capital upfront, real estate offers tangible assets that often act as a hedge

against inflation. Properties can be residential, commercial, or even vacation rentals, each with unique benefits and challenges. For those unable to purchase physical property, real estate investment trusts (REITs) provide an accessible way to benefit from the real estate market without the need for direct management.

- **Mutual Funds and ETFs**: These pooled investments allow you to buy a basket of assets, providing instant diversification. ETFs (Exchange-Traded Funds) often track an index and come with lower fees, making them ideal for beginners. Mutual funds are actively managed and may have higher fees but offer professional oversight. Both options are excellent for those who prefer a hands-off approach to investing while still accessing diversified portfolios.

- **Cryptocurrency**: Digital currencies like Bitcoin and Ethereum have captured global attention. While they offer high potential returns, they're highly speculative and volatile, requiring careful consideration. Cryptocurrencies operate outside traditional financial systems, and their value is often driven by market sentiment, technological developments, and regulatory changes. They can be a small, high-risk portion of a diversified portfolio for those willing to embrace uncertainty.

- **Commodities**: Physical goods like gold, oil, or agricultural products can serve as a hedge against economic uncertainty. Commodities are often used to diversify portfolios but can be influenced by geopolitical and market conditions. Gold, for instance, is considered a safe haven during times of economic instability, while oil prices fluctuate with global supply and demand dynamics.

How to Get Started

Starting your investment journey doesn't require a fortune. What it does require is intention and consistency. The earlier you begin, the more time your money has to grow. Here's how to lay the groundwork:

Set clear goals that align with your life aspirations. Are you investing for retirement, buying a home, or funding a future child's education? Knowing your destination helps shape your investment strategy.

Evaluate your risk tolerance. Ask yourself how much uncertainty you're comfortable with. Younger investors can often take on more risk since they have time to recover from downturns. Older investors may prioritize stability to protect their wealth.

Choose the right platform. Online brokers and investment apps have revolutionized the way people invest, making it more accessible and straightforward for beginners and seasoned investors alike. These platforms often come with user-friendly interfaces that guide you through the investment process, whether you're purchasing your first stock or diversifying your portfolio. Low fees are a critical factor to consider, as excessive costs can eat into your returns over time. Platforms that charge lower transaction fees or offer commission-free trading can significantly enhance your long-term gains.

Additionally, many modern investment platforms provide a wealth of educational resources tailored to users at different stages of their investing journey. These resources may include articles, tutorials, webinars, and even simulation tools that allow you to practice investing without risking real money. Some platforms also offer financial planning tools that help you align your investment choices with your overall financial goals, whether you're saving for retirement, a home, or a major life event.

Another feature to evaluate is the range of investment options available. A good platform should offer access to a broad spectrum of assets, such as stocks, bonds, ETFs, mutual funds, and even alternative investments like cryptocurrencies or REITs. This diversity allows you to build a balanced portfolio that matches your risk tolerance and investment objectives.

Finally, consider customer support and accessibility. Reliable platforms should provide responsive customer service to address your questions or issues promptly. Mobile app functionality is another advantage, allowing you to monitor and manage your investments on the go. By choosing the right platform, you set the stage for a seamless and informed investing experience, ensuring your money works efficiently for you.

Start small but stay consistent. Even if you can only invest a small amount initially, regular contributions add up over time. Automating your investments ensures you stay disciplined, regardless of market conditions.

Educate yourself continuously. Read books, follow financial experts, and keep up with market trends. The more knowledge you have, the better equipped you'll be to navigate the investing landscape.

The Power of Patience

One of the most critical aspects of investing is patience. Markets fluctuate, sometimes dramatically, and it's important to remember that these ups and downs are a natural part of the investment journey. It can be tempting to react emotionally during periods of market volatility, selling when prices dip or trying to time the market to maximize gains. However, history shows that the most successful investors are those who stay the course and allow time to do the heavy lifting.

Patience in investing isn't about passivity; it's about trusting your strategy and making informed decisions. Markets have historically trended upward over the long term, despite short-term downturns and occasional recessions. For instance, consider major market indices like the S&P 500 or the FTSE 100. While they have experienced significant drops during crises, such as the 2008 financial crash or the COVID-19 pandemic, they have always recovered and reached new heights. Investors who remained patient and avoided panic selling during these times were ultimately rewarded for their resilience.

Compound growth is one of the key reasons patience is so vital. When you stay invested, your returns begin to generate their own returns, creating a snowball effect that accelerates over time. This is especially true for those who start investing early and maintain their positions for decades. Even during years when market performance is underwhelming, the compounding process continues to build wealth in the background, laying the foundation for substantial future gains.

Another aspect of patience is recognizing that not all investments will perform well immediately. Some stocks or funds may take years to realize their potential, particularly in industries that are emerging or undergoing transformation. Investors who understand this dynamic are less likely to abandon promising opportunities prematurely. Patience gives your investments the time they need to grow and mature, allowing you to capture their full value.

Patience also helps mitigate the emotional stress that can come with investing. When you adopt a long-term perspective, you're less likely to be swayed by daily market movements or sensational headlines predicting doom and gloom. Instead, you can focus on your broader financial goals and trust in the strategies you've put in place. This mindset not only improves your financial outcomes but also fosters a healthier relationship with money.

Lastly, patience allows you to take advantage of opportunities that arise during market downturns. When prices fall, disciplined investors view it as a chance to buy quality assets at a discount, knowing that these investments are likely to recover and grow in value over time. This approach, often referred to as "buying the dip," requires confidence and a willingness to go against the crowd. However, it's a proven strategy for building wealth and reinforcing the importance of staying the course.

In summary, patience is one of the most powerful tools in an investor's arsenal. By resisting the urge to react impulsively to market fluctuations, focusing on the long term, and allowing your investments to compound and grow, you position yourself for success. Investing is not a get-rich-quick scheme; it's a journey that rewards those who have the discipline and fortitude to see it through.

Compound Interest: The Snowball Effect

Compound interest is one of the most transformative forces in personal finance and investing. It works like a snowball rolling downhill, growing larger and faster as it accumulates more snow. The idea is simple: when you invest money, you earn returns on your initial investment. Over time, those returns start earning their own returns, creating a compounding effect that accelerates your wealth-building journey.

The earlier you start harnessing compound interest, the more powerful its effects become. For example, investing £10,000 at a 7% annual return would grow to nearly £20,000 in just 10 years. But over 30 years, that same initial amount balloons to almost £80,000 without any additional contributions. This exponential growth happens because each year's returns are reinvested, building a foundation for even greater returns in subsequent years.

Small, consistent actions can yield massive rewards over time. Consider someone who invests £200 per month starting at age 25. Assuming a 7% annual return, their investment would grow to over £245,000 by age 55. By continuing these contributions until age 65, the total swells to more than £515,000. This demonstrates how modest contributions, combined with time and reinvestment, can lead to substantial wealth.

Now imagine starting just ten years later at age 35. Even with the same monthly contributions and rate of return, the investment would grow to only around £245,000 by age 65. This significant difference illustrates the critical role time plays in harnessing the power of compound interest. Starting earlier not only gives your investments more time to grow but also allows compounding to work its magic over a longer horizon, multiplying the benefits exponentially.

It's not just the initial contributions that matter; reinvesting your returns is equally critical. For example, the interest or dividends earned on your investments should ideally be reinvested rather than withdrawn. Reinvestment accelerates the compounding process, ensuring that every penny contributes to further growth. Over decades, this approach can turn modest contributions into a substantial financial safety net or even generational wealth.

The discipline to invest consistently is vital. Market fluctuations and economic uncertainties may create a temptation to pause contributions or withdraw funds. However, maintaining a steady pace of investing during both high and low periods allows you to take advantage of market dips, purchasing assets at lower prices. This dollar-cost averaging strategy helps smooth out the effects of market volatility and maximizes long-term growth.

It's important to note that compounding works best when left uninterrupted. Frequent withdrawals or selling investments can disrupt the compounding process, significantly reducing your potential gains. This is why long-term thinking is critical to maximizing the benefits of compound interest.

At its core, compound interest is driven by time, rate of return, and consistency. The longer your money stays invested, the more opportunities it has to grow. Higher rates of return also amplify the effects of compounding, though they often come with greater risk. Consistency, even during market downturns, ensures that your investment continues to build over time.

Understanding the role of interest rates is essential when discussing compounding. Central banks, such as the Bank of England or the Federal Reserve, play a pivotal role in setting interest rates that ripple across the broader economy, influencing everything from individual borrowing costs to global investment strategies. When central banks lower interest rates, borrowing becomes more affordable, spurring individuals and businesses to take out loans for activities like home purchases, business expansions, and investment in growth opportunities. This increased borrowing often drives economic activity and can lead to higher valuations in equities and real estate as capital flows more freely.

Conversely, higher interest rates are used by central banks to cool down inflation or an overheating economy. These higher rates make borrowing more expensive, discouraging both personal and corporate loans. However, they can be a boon for savers, as fixed-income investments like bonds and savings accounts tend to offer better returns in a high-interest-rate environment. For investors, rising rates can shift the attractiveness of asset classes. While stocks might experience downward pressure due to higher borrowing costs for companies, bonds and other fixed-income instruments often become more appealing.

Understanding these dynamics is crucial for investors aiming to optimize their portfolios. During periods of low interest rates, growth-oriented investments such as stocks and real estate typically thrive due to cheaper access to capital. Meanwhile, in high-rate environments, conservative investments like government bonds and high-yield savings accounts may offer more secure returns. By staying attuned to central bank policies and their rationale, such as tackling inflation or stimulating economic growth, investors can make more informed decisions about reallocating assets to suit the prevailing economic conditions.

For individual investors, the impact of central bank policies trickles down into everything from mortgage rates to the performance of bonds and equities. Low interest rates often drive people toward stocks and other higher-yield investments, as borrowing becomes cheaper and companies find it easier to expand. This environment often leads to a surge in real estate investments as well, as lower mortgage rates make home ownership and property investments more accessible.

Conversely, high interest rates can shift the focus to fixed-income assets like bonds and savings accounts, which become more lucrative due to their improved returns. Savers benefit from higher rates, as their deposits earn more interest over time. For instance, a high-interest-rate environment might see savings accounts offering returns that are competitive with low-risk bonds, making them appealing for those seeking stability.

Understanding these dynamics allows individual investors to anticipate market shifts and adjust their strategies accordingly. For example, during periods of low interest rates, growth-oriented assets like technology stocks and emerging markets might outperform, while during periods of high rates, value stocks and dividend-paying companies often hold greater appeal. Moreover, real estate investments might slow down when borrowing costs rise, but bonds and treasury securities tend to see increased demand as they offer safer, predictable returns.

Staying attuned to central bank policies also provides insight into broader economic trends, such as inflation, currency valuation, and overall economic growth. Recognizing how these factors interplay with interest rates can help investors diversify their portfolios effectively and seize opportunities that align with the prevailing economic climate. For instance, during an aggressive rate-hiking cycle, maintaining a balanced portfolio with exposure to both equities and high-yield fixed-income products can help mitigate risk while still providing growth potential.

In conclusion, central bank policies are more than abstract economic tools; they are direct influencers of everyday investment decisions. By understanding the cascading effects of these policies, investors can make more strategic choices about asset allocation, timing, and overall portfolio management, ensuring long-term financial resilience and growth.

In summary, compound interest is a remarkable phenomenon that rewards patience, consistency, and a long-term perspective. By understanding how it works and staying disciplined in your approach, you can harness its power to achieve your financial goals while navigating the broader economic landscape influenced by central bank policies."

Multiple Income Streams: Beyond the 9-to-5

Relying solely on a 9-to-5 job as your only source of income can feel secure, but it also leaves you vulnerable to financial instability if unexpected events arise, such as layoffs or economic downturns. Diversifying your income streams is a key strategy to not only safeguard against such uncertainties but also to accelerate your journey toward financial independence. Building multiple revenue streams takes time and effort, but the long-term rewards are well worth it.

One of the most accessible ways to create an additional income stream is through side hustles. These can range from freelance work and consulting to creative pursuits like selling handmade crafts, starting an online business, or even offering specialized services such as tutoring or photography. Thanks to digital platforms like Etsy, Upwork, Fiverr, and social media marketplaces, turning a skill or passion into a source of income has never been easier. These platforms not only connect you with a global audience but also provide tools to showcase your expertise and attract clients.

The beauty of side hustles is their flexibility; they allow you to earn extra money without abandoning your primary job. For example, a teacher might offer private tutoring sessions in the evenings, or an artist might sell commissioned artwork during weekends. These endeavors can fit around your existing schedule, making them accessible to anyone willing to put in the effort. Initially, the income might be small, covering minor expenses or adding a little extra cushion to your monthly budget. However, consistent effort and dedication can turn these ventures into significant sources of revenue over time.

Building a successful side hustle often involves refining your craft, marketing your services, and maintaining excellent customer relationships. While it takes time to gain traction, many individuals find that their side hustles evolve into primary income streams or even full-fledged businesses. For instance, a hobbyist who starts baking cakes for friends might grow their passion into a thriving catering business with consistent orders and a loyal customer base. The possibilities are vast, limited only by creativity and commitment.

Another powerful way to diversify income is through passive income streams. Investments in stocks, bonds, real estate, or even dividend-paying mutual funds can generate regular returns with minimal ongoing effort. For example, owning rental properties provides steady income while the property itself appreciates in value. Similarly, dividend-paying stocks offer payouts simply for holding shares in established companies. While passive income often requires upfront capital, its potential to provide long-term financial stability and freedom is unparalleled.

Creating digital products or content is another avenue to explore. Writing an eBook, developing an online course, or monetizing a YouTube channel are examples of ventures that can generate income while requiring only maintenance once the initial work is done. Although building an audience and creating valuable content takes time, these projects can become significant income streams over time, especially if they address niche markets or solve specific problems for your audience.

Time is a critical factor in building multiple income streams. Each venture, whether active or passive, requires an initial investment of energy, resources, and patience. These streams are not instantaneous solutions; they demand sustained effort and a long-term vision. Whether it's starting a small business, creating digital products, or investing in income-generating assets, the process of establishing and growing these streams often involves a steep learning curve and numerous trial-and-error experiences.

It's important to approach these endeavors with realistic expectations, understanding that success doesn't happen overnight. For example, a side hustle like freelance graphic design might begin with only a few clients but can grow steadily over months and years as you build your portfolio and reputation. Similarly, investments in dividend-paying stocks or rental properties might yield modest returns initially, but with reinvestment and time, they can develop into reliable sources of income.

Persistence is key. The cumulative effect of having multiple income sources can drastically improve your financial situation over time. As one stream grows, it can complement or even feed into others, creating a compounding effect that accelerates your journey toward financial independence. For instance, profits from a small online business could be reinvested into real estate or the stock market, diversifying your portfolio and amplifying your overall returns.

Over time, these streams can grow to rival or even surpass the income from your primary job, providing greater financial stability and freedom. This diversification also reduces your reliance on a single paycheck, mitigating risks associated with job loss or economic downturns. With patience, consistent effort, and a willingness to adapt, multiple income streams can transform your financial landscape, giving you more options and security for the future.

Moreover, diversifying your income teaches valuable lessons about resilience and adaptability. Each new venture expands your skillset, builds your network, and increases your financial literacy. These benefits compound over time, making you more resourceful and better prepared to navigate the uncertainties of life and work.

Growing a business is an entirely different undertaking from merely starting a side hustle or pursuing additional income streams. It demands not just time but also strategic planning, relentless effort, and a willingness to face risks and challenges. Building a company requires a solid foundation, starting with a clear vision and mission. This vision not only guides the direction of the business but also serves as the driving force behind every decision.

In the early stages, most businesses operate with limited resources, requiring founders to wear multiple hats. You may find yourself acting as the marketer, accountant, product developer, and customer service representative all at once. Long hours and sacrifices become the norm as you dedicate your energy to establishing your brand, attracting customers, and delivering quality products or services. Success rarely comes overnight; instead, it is the result of consistent effort, learning from failures, and adapting to market demands.

One of the most significant challenges in growing a business is managing cash flow. Maintaining a balance between reinvesting profits into the business and keeping it financially stable can be tricky. Entrepreneurs must learn to budget effectively, negotiate better terms with suppliers, and seek out funding opportunities such as loans, grants, or investor backing when necessary. These financial decisions often determine whether a business thrives or struggles to stay afloat.

Marketing and building a customer base are equally critical. In today's digital age, having a strong online presence is essential. This involves creating a professional website, leveraging social media platforms, and employing digital marketing strategies like search engine optimization (SEO) and pay-per-click advertising. Engaging with your audience, gathering feedback, and building customer loyalty are vital for establishing a reputable brand and ensuring repeat business.

As the business grows, scaling becomes the next major hurdle. Scaling requires hiring the right team, investing in efficient systems, and streamlining operations to handle increased demand. Delegation becomes key, as no entrepreneur can do it all alone. Hiring skilled employees who align with your company's values can make a significant difference in the long-term success of your business. Training and empowering your team ensures that the company can function smoothly even as you shift your focus to strategic planning and growth.

Patience and perseverance are essential throughout the journey of growing a business. It may take years before you see significant returns, and the path is often filled with setbacks, learning curves, and unforeseen challenges. Building a business is not just about monetary gain; it's about growth, both personal and professional. The process demands relentless effort and an unwavering belief in your vision, even when progress seems slow or obstacles appear insurmountable.

Every setback presents an opportunity to learn and adapt. Whether it's refining your business model, rethinking your marketing strategy, or identifying new customer needs, these moments of growth often define the trajectory of your company. Success rarely comes in a linear fashion; it's more often the result of countless iterations, small wins, and moments of resilience in the face of adversity. For example, a product launch that initially fails might lead you to identify a better market fit or improve your offering—transforming a challenge into an advantage.

Time is a crucial component in this journey. Many successful businesses that appear to be overnight successes are, in reality, the result of years of behind-the-scenes effort. Milestones such as acquiring your first major client, achieving profitability, or scaling to new markets don't happen without countless hours of dedication and a willingness to keep pushing forward. Each of these accomplishments serves as a powerful reminder of how far you've come and reinforces the value of your hard work.

The potential for financial independence makes the effort worthwhile. A thriving business provides more than just a steady income; it offers freedom—freedom to make decisions on your own terms, to pursue your passions, and to create a legacy that can outlast you. Moreover, the sense of accomplishment that comes from seeing your vision come to life and making an impact in your industry or community is invaluable. Growing a business is not just about the destination but the journey itself, and every step along the way shapes you into a stronger, more capable entrepreneur.

In conclusion, multiple income streams are not just a financial strategy but a mindset shift. By stepping beyond the confines of a single paycheck and exploring creative ways to earn, you position yourself for greater financial stability, freedom, and growth. The path to building these streams may take time, but the rewards—both tangible and intangible—are life-changing.

Part 4: Reaching Financial Freedom

Breaking Free from Golden Handcuffs: The Exit Plan

Escaping a high-paying but soul-draining job to achieve real freedom is a challenge that requires courage, planning, and a clear understanding of what true fulfillment looks like for you. Golden handcuffs refer to the trap of staying in a lucrative yet unsatisfying career because of the financial comfort it provides. While the paychecks may be rewarding, the cost to your mental health, personal relationships, and overall happiness can be immense. Breaking free from this cycle is not about recklessly quitting but creating a thoughtful exit plan that prioritizes both financial security and personal well-being.

The first step in the exit plan is redefining what success means to you. Many individuals equate success with a high income or prestigious job title, but these markers often fail to provide lasting satisfaction. True success is deeply personal and extends beyond monetary wealth or professional accolades. It requires an honest evaluation of what genuinely brings you happiness and fulfillment. Take time to reflect on your values, passions, and long-term goals. Ask yourself what activities energize and excite you, and consider the type of lifestyle you wish to lead. Is it one filled with flexibility, creativity, or meaningful connections? Understanding these elements is crucial in creating a vision for your future that feels authentic and sustainable.

Redefining success also means challenging societal norms and expectations that may have influenced your career choices. Many people feel pressure to pursue traditional paths or remain in high-status roles due to external validation. Breaking free from this mindset involves embracing the idea that your worth isn't tied to your job title or paycheck but to how well your life aligns with your core values. For example, someone who values family time might define success as having a career that allows for a flexible schedule, even if it means earning less. Similarly, someone passionate about creative expression might prioritize a role in the arts over a corporate position, despite the financial trade-offs.

This process of redefinition requires introspection and may involve experimenting with different interests to discover what resonates most with you. Journaling, speaking with mentors, or engaging in activities outside your comfort zone can help uncover insights into what truly matters. As you gain clarity, you'll be better equipped to identify opportunities that align with your unique vision of success, setting the foundation for a purposeful and fulfilling transition.

Financial preparation is key to making a smooth transition. Start by building a robust savings cushion that can cover your expenses for at least six months to a year. This safety net reduces the pressure of needing immediate income after leaving your job, allowing you to explore new opportunities with less stress. Additionally, evaluate your current expenses and identify areas where you can cut back. Living below your means during this transition can stretch your savings and give you more time to find your footing.

Exploring alternative income streams is another crucial part of the process. Consider side hustles, freelancing, or starting a small business while still employed. These ventures not only provide extra income but also give you a chance to test new career paths without fully committing. For instance, if you've always dreamed of becoming a writer, start by freelancing or publishing online. If entrepreneurship appeals to you, begin by offering a product or service on a small scale. Over time, these efforts can grow into sustainable income sources that allow you to leave your current job with confidence.

Networking and skill-building are equally important. Expanding your professional network can open doors to opportunities you might not have considered. Attend industry events, join online communities, and reach out to mentors who can provide guidance and support. Simultaneously, invest in developing skills relevant to your desired career path. This could involve taking courses, earning certifications, or gaining hands-on experience through volunteer work or internships.

Emotional preparation is often overlooked but is just as critical as financial and professional readiness. Leaving a high-paying job can bring a whirlwind of emotions—fear of financial insecurity, uncertainty about the future, and even guilt over walking away from a role others might envy. It's important to acknowledge these feelings and address them constructively rather than suppressing them. Recognize that these emotions are a natural part of making a significant life change.

One of the most effective ways to navigate these emotional challenges is to surround yourself with supportive people who understand your decision and can offer encouragement. These might include close friends, family members, or mentors who can provide a sounding board for your concerns and remind you of the reasons behind your decision. Joining communities of like-minded individuals who have also made similar transitions can be especially empowering. Hearing their stories of struggle and eventual success can provide reassurance that you're not alone and that the path you're choosing is both valid and achievable.

Remind yourself constantly of your reasons for leaving and the long-term benefits of pursuing a path that aligns with your passions and values. Create a list of personal affirmations or goals that keep you focused on why this transition is necessary for your happiness and well-being. Reflecting on how this change aligns with your deeper sense of purpose can help counteract doubts and reinforce your commitment.

It's also helpful to set realistic expectations for the emotional journey ahead. Understand that you might experience moments of doubt, nostalgia for the financial comfort you once had, or anxiety about the challenges of building something new. Preparing for these feelings in advance can reduce their impact and help you cope when they arise. Consider working with a coach or therapist to develop strategies for managing stress and maintaining your emotional resilience during this period of uncertainty.

Ultimately, emotional preparation is about fortifying your mindset to embrace change with confidence and optimism. It's not about eliminating fear entirely but learning how to move forward despite it, trusting that the rewards of living a life aligned with your passions and values will far outweigh the temporary discomfort of letting go of the familiar.

Finally, create a detailed timeline for your transition. Setting clear milestones and deadlines is crucial to maintaining focus and ensuring accountability throughout the process. Start by identifying key objectives that align with your overall exit strategy. For example, this might include saving a specific amount of money to cover living expenses for six months to a year, researching alternative career paths, or launching a side business within a specific timeframe. Breaking these goals into smaller, actionable steps makes the transition feel less overwhelming and allows you to track your progress more effectively.

Consider dividing your timeline into short-term, medium-term, and long-term goals. In the short term, focus on immediate actions such as reducing unnecessary expenses, increasing your savings rate, or taking the first steps to build a professional network in your desired field. Medium-term goals might involve enrolling in a course to upskill, developing a portfolio or resume tailored to your new career, or testing a side hustle to gauge its potential viability. Long-term goals could include securing a position in your new field, scaling your side business to a sustainable level, or achieving a financial milestone that gives you the confidence to leave your current role.

Regularly reviewing and adjusting your timeline is just as important as setting it. Life circumstances, economic conditions, or even new insights about your goals can influence your progress, so staying flexible is key. Schedule monthly or quarterly check-ins to evaluate your achievements, identify any challenges, and revise your plan as necessary. This iterative process not only keeps you on track but also reinforces your commitment to the transition.

Incorporating rewards for meeting milestones can also boost motivation. Celebrate small victories, like successfully saving your first few months of living expenses or landing your first client in a new venture. These moments of recognition serve as reminders of how far you've come and encourage you to keep moving forward.

Breaking free from golden handcuffs is not an easy decision, but it's a transformative one that can redefine your relationship with work, money, and life itself. It requires a strategic and holistic approach that carefully balances practical steps with a deep commitment to self-discovery. This journey is not simply about walking away from a paycheck; it's about reclaiming control over your time, energy, and passions to create a life that aligns with your core values and long-term goals.

True freedom often comes with sacrifices and resilience. It might mean cutting back on luxuries you once took for granted or stepping into the uncertainty of an unfamiliar career path. Yet, with effort and perseverance, these challenges can become stepping stones to a more fulfilling existence. The process of breaking free forces you to confront fears, question societal expectations, and push beyond comfort zones, but in doing so, it fosters personal growth and strengthens your resolve.

The rewards of this journey extend beyond financial considerations. They include the freedom to pursue work that feels meaningful, the opportunity to spend more quality time with loved ones, and the ability to design a lifestyle that prioritizes your well-being and happiness. It's about finding purpose in your everyday life and knowing that the decisions you make reflect your authentic self. Each step you take in this process, no matter how small, brings you closer to a life defined not by external pressures but by what truly matters to you.

While the path to breaking free from golden handcuffs can be daunting, it is ultimately a path toward empowerment and self-fulfillment. By staying committed to your vision, leveraging your strengths, and remaining adaptable in the face of challenges, you can achieve a freedom that transcends financial gain. The journey may demand patience and persistence, but the reward—a life lived on your own terms—is worth every moment of effort.

Your Financial Freedom Plan: GPS to Your Goals

Achieving financial independence is a journey that requires a clear and well-thought-out roadmap. Much like using GPS to navigate an unfamiliar destination, your financial freedom plan should provide direction, highlight potential detours, and ensure you stay on track toward your goals. This process starts with defining what financial independence means to you. For some, it's about retiring early and living off passive income; for others, it might mean having the freedom to pursue creative passions without financial stress or starting a business without fear of failure.

Begin by setting specific, measurable goals that align with your vision of financial independence. Break these goals into short-term, medium-term, and long-term objectives. For example, short-term goals might include creating a budget, building an emergency fund, or paying off high-interest debt. Medium-term goals could involve saving for a home, investing in your education, or starting to contribute regularly to a retirement account. Long-term goals often center around building substantial wealth, achieving full financial independence, and leaving a legacy for your family or community.

Once you've defined your goals, the next step is to assess your current financial situation. Take a comprehensive inventory of your income, expenses, debts, and assets. This evaluation provides a baseline from which to plan your journey. Understanding where you stand financially helps identify areas for improvement and opportunities for growth. For instance, you may discover that reducing discretionary spending could free up funds for investment, or that consolidating debt could accelerate your progress toward financial freedom.

Developing a detailed budget is an essential part of this process. A budget acts as your financial compass, guiding how you allocate resources toward achieving your goals. Prioritize saving and investing over unnecessary expenditures, and automate these processes whenever possible to ensure consistency. Even small, regular contributions to savings or investment accounts can grow significantly over time thanks to the power of compounding.

Investing is a cornerstone of any financial freedom plan. Ensure that your investment strategy aligns with your goals and risk tolerance. Diversify your portfolio to reduce risk and maximize returns, and take advantage of tax-advantaged accounts such as ISAs or 401(k)s to accelerate your wealth-building efforts. Regularly review and adjust your investments to stay aligned with your evolving goals and market conditions.

Eliminating debt is another critical milestone on the road to financial independence. High-interest debts, such as credit card balances, can erode your ability to save and invest. Develop a repayment strategy that prioritizes these obligations while maintaining steady contributions to your savings and investments. Consider the snowball or avalanche method for paying off debt—both are effective strategies that cater to different psychological and financial preferences.

Building multiple income streams is also instrumental in creating financial stability and accelerating your journey to independence. Explore opportunities such as side hustles, freelancing, or passive income ventures like rental properties or dividend investing. Each additional income stream not only increases your financial security but also shortens the time it takes to reach your ultimate goals.

As you progress, regularly monitor your plan and celebrate milestones along the way. Financial independence is a long-term pursuit, and maintaining motivation is essential. Acknowledge your achievements, whether it's paying off a significant debt, reaching a savings milestone, or successfully launching a side business. These moments of success reinforce the effectiveness of your plan and keep you focused on the bigger picture.

Remember, a financial freedom plan is not static. Life circumstances, goals, and economic conditions change, and your plan should evolve accordingly. Stay flexible and open to new opportunities that align with your vision, and don't hesitate to seek guidance from financial advisors or mentors when needed.

Ultimately, your financial freedom plan is your personal guide to a life of choice and opportunity. By following this roadmap with discipline and adaptability, you can navigate the complexities of personal finance and create a future defined by freedom, security, and fulfillment.

Part 5: Navigating Taxation and Maximizing Savings

Taxes Demystified: Don't Let the Brackets Fool You

Understanding taxes can feel overwhelming, but having a clear grasp of how tax brackets work in the UK and USA can significantly improve your financial planning. At their core, tax brackets are designed to tax income progressively, meaning higher earnings are taxed at higher rates. However, many people misunderstand how these brackets function, leading to unnecessary stress or even financial missteps.

In the UK, tax brackets apply progressively, meaning you only pay the specified rate on the portion of your income that falls within each bracket. This ensures fairness, as your entire income is not taxed at the highest rate you qualify for. To illustrate, let's break down the current brackets (as of 2024):

- **Personal Allowance**: The first £12,570 of your income is tax-free. For example, if you earn £12,000 annually, you won't pay any income tax.
- **Basic Rate**: Income between £12,571 and £50,270 is taxed at 20%. If your salary is £40,000, you'll pay 20% only on the portion above £12,570, which amounts to £27,430.
- **Higher Rate**: Income between £50,271 and £125,140 is taxed at 40%. For instance, if you earn £60,000 annually, you'll pay 40% on the £9,730 that exceeds the basic-rate threshold.
- **Additional Rate**: Income above £125,140 is taxed at 45%. For example, if your annual salary is £130,000, only the £4,860 above £125,140 is taxed at 45%.

Understanding this structure is vital for accurate financial planning and avoiding common misconceptions. For instance, someone earning £60,000 may mistakenly believe their entire salary is taxed at the higher rate of 40%, leading to unnecessary financial stress or even poor financial decisions. In reality, only the portion of their income above £50,270 is taxed at 40%, while the rest is subject to lower rates—20% on income between £12,571 and £50,270, and no tax on the first £12,570 due to the personal allowance. This progressive system ensures fairness but requires careful understanding to optimize financial outcomes.

To further enhance your financial planning, strategic actions like contributing to a pension or an ISA can significantly reduce your taxable income. Pension contributions, for example, are deducted before income tax is calculated, allowing you to lower your effective tax rate while securing your future. For higher-rate taxpayers, contributing additional funds to a pension plan can even bring their income back into the basic-rate band, saving thousands of pounds annually. Similarly, ISAs offer a tax-free environment for both savings and investments, ensuring that any interest, dividends, or capital gains remain untaxed, regardless of your income level.

By leveraging these tools, you not only optimize your tax position but also build a robust financial foundation for the future. Whether through careful salary structuring, strategic use of tax-advantaged accounts, or taking advantage of allowances like the marriage allowance or rent-a-room relief, understanding the nuances of the tax system empowers you to make informed decisions that maximize your wealth and minimize liabilities over time.

Capital Gains Tax in the UK

Capital gains tax (CGT) in the UK is a tax on the profit when you sell or dispose of an asset that has increased in value. It is not the total sale price that is taxed, but the gain you have made. Understanding how CGT works is essential for effective financial planning, especially if you are an investor, property owner, or business operator.

As of 2024, the UK provides an annual tax-free allowance for capital gains. For individuals, this allowance is £6,000, meaning you can make gains up to this amount without paying any tax. However, gains exceeding this threshold are subject to taxation based on your income tax band.

- **Basic Rate Taxpayers**: If your total income and gains (minus allowances) place you in the basic income tax band, you pay 10% CGT on most assets and 18% on residential property gains.
- **Higher and Additional Rate Taxpayers**: If your total income and gains exceed the basic rate threshold, you pay 20% CGT on most assets and 28% on residential property gains.

For example, suppose you are a basic rate taxpayer earning £40,000 annually and sell shares for a £12,000 gain. After deducting the £6,000 allowance, the remaining £6,000 is taxable. Since your total income and gains remain within the basic rate band, you would pay 10% of £6,000, which equals £600. Conversely, a higher-rate taxpayer making the same gain would pay 20%, resulting in a £1,200 tax bill.

Property sales are treated differently, particularly for second homes or rental properties. Suppose you sell a rental property with a £25,000 gain after deducting allowable expenses. If you are a higher-rate taxpayer, the first £6,000 is tax-free, leaving £19,000 taxable at 28%. This results in a CGT liability of £5,320.

CGT also applies to the disposal of business assets, though entrepreneurs may benefit from Business Asset Disposal Relief (formerly Entrepreneurs' Relief). This reduces the CGT rate to 10% on qualifying gains, subject to a lifetime limit of £1 million.

Strategies to minimize CGT include:

- Utilizing the annual allowance by spreading disposals across tax years.
- Offsetting gains with allowable losses from other assets.
- Holding assets in tax-advantaged accounts like ISAs, where gains are entirely exempt from CGT.

By understanding how CGT works and leveraging available allowances and reliefs, you can effectively manage your tax liabilities and maximize your wealth.

USA Tax

Understanding the U.S. federal income tax brackets provides critical insight into how your earnings are taxed and helps with financial planning. Federal income tax is progressive, meaning different portions of your income are taxed at different rates. As of 2024, here's a breakdown:

- **10% Bracket**: This applies to the first $11,000 of taxable income for single filers or $22,000 for married couples filing jointly. For example, if you earn $10,000, your entire income is taxed at this rate.
- **12% Bracket**: Income between $11,001 and $44,725 for single filers, or $22,001 to $89,450 for joint filers. For instance, if you earn $30,000 as a single filer, you'll pay 10% on the first $11,000 and 12% on the remaining $19,000.

- **22% Bracket**: Income between $44,726 and $95,375 for single filers, or $89,451 to $190,750 for joint filers. If your salary is $60,000, you'll pay 10% on the first $11,000, 12% on the next $33,725, and 22% on the remaining $15,275.
- **24% Bracket**: Income between $95,376 and $182,100 for single filers, or $190,751 to $364,200 for joint filers. For example, if you earn $120,000 as a single filer, only the income between $95,376 and $120,000 is taxed at 24%.
- **32% Bracket**: Income between $182,101 and $231,250 for single filers, or $364,201 to $462,500 for joint filers.
- **35% Bracket**: Income between $231,251 and $578,125 for single filers, or $462,501 to $693,750 for joint filers.
- **37% Bracket**: Income above $578,126 for single filers, or $693,751 for joint filers.

By understanding this structure, you can accurately calculate your effective tax rate, which is typically much lower than your highest marginal rate due to the progressive system. For example, a single filer earning $80,000 doesn't pay 22% on their entire income; they pay progressively higher rates on portions of their income within each bracket.

Contributing to tax-advantaged accounts, such as a 401(k) or an IRA, can reduce your taxable income by shifting earnings into these accounts before taxes are calculated. For instance, a $5,000 contribution to a 401(k) reduces a $60,000 salary to $55,000 for tax purposes, potentially lowering the portion of income taxed at higher rates. Similarly, using deductions and credits can further reduce tax liability, maximizing your overall tax efficiency while setting aside funds for the future.

How Understanding Taxes Can Help You Keep More of Your Money

By learning how different types of income are taxed, you can make smarter financial decisions and strategically plan for long-term wealth. In the UK, income from dividends or capital gains is often taxed at lower rates than employment income, making investments a powerful tool for growing wealth. For example, the UK's capital gains tax allows basic-rate taxpayers to pay just 10% on their investment gains, compared to the 20% rate applied to most forms of earned income. This favorable tax treatment encourages investors to prioritize assets with growth potential, such as stocks or real estate.

Similarly, in the USA, long-term capital gains—defined as gains on investments held for over a year—enjoy preferential tax rates compared to regular income. These rates range from 0% for individuals with taxable income under $44,625 (single filers) to a maximum of 20% for high-income earners. For example, an investor earning $50,000 who realizes $10,000 in long-term capital gains would pay a 15% tax on those gains, significantly lower than the ordinary income tax rate that would apply to short-term gains or wages. This incentivizes a buy-and-hold strategy, encouraging investors to think long-term rather than engaging in short-term speculation.

Understanding these distinctions allows individuals to craft tax-efficient strategies. For instance, UK investors can make use of tax-free allowances like the £6,000 annual exemption on capital gains, while U.S. taxpayers can employ tax-loss harvesting to offset gains with losses, thereby reducing their taxable income further. Whether through structured investments, maximizing allowances, or holding assets for longer periods, taking advantage of these opportunities can significantly enhance your financial outcomes.

Understanding deductions and credits is equally crucial for optimizing your financial situation and minimizing your tax liability. In the UK, deductions such as claiming work-from-home expenses, contributions to pension plans, or charitable donations can significantly reduce your taxable income. For instance, if you contribute to a workplace pension under a salary sacrifice arrangement, the contributions are deducted before income tax is calculated, allowing you to save more effectively for retirement while lowering your immediate tax burden. Similarly, higher-rate taxpayers can claim additional tax relief on contributions to private pension schemes, further incentivizing long-term savings.

In the USA, deductions like student loan interest or state and local tax (SALT) payments can substantially reduce your taxable income. Tax credits, such as the Child Tax Credit or the Earned Income Tax Credit (EITC), directly lower the amount of tax owed and are particularly valuable. For example, a family eligible for the Child Tax Credit could reduce their tax bill by up to $2,000 per qualifying child. Unlike deductions, which reduce taxable income, credits provide dollar-for-dollar reductions in tax liability, making them highly impactful.

Maintaining accurate and detailed financial records is essential for leveraging these opportunities fully. Keep receipts, invoices, and documentation of charitable contributions, educational expenses, and medical costs, as these may qualify for deductions or credits. Investing in accounting software or working with a tax professional ensures that you stay compliant while maximizing the benefits available to you under tax law. A tax expert can also help identify less obvious deductions and credits, ensuring you're not leaving money on the table.

Additionally, understanding the nuances of these benefits allows you to plan strategically throughout the year. For instance, in the UK, deferring income to a future tax year or spreading charitable donations across multiple years can help keep your taxable income within a lower bracket. Similarly, in the USA, bunching itemized deductions into a single year or leveraging Health Savings Accounts (HSAs) for tax-free medical expenses are effective strategies for reducing your overall tax burden. By proactively managing your finances with these tools in mind, you can significantly improve your financial outcomes while building long-term wealth.

Understanding and optimizing your taxes is not just about compliance; it's about taking control of your financial future. By demystifying the process, leveraging available tools, and seeking expert advice when needed, you can ensure you keep more of your hard-earned money while building a secure financial foundation.

Part 6: Securing Long-Term Stability Insurance

Protecting Your Wealth: Insurance and Safeguards

Building wealth is a significant achievement, but protecting it is just as important. Without safeguards in place, unexpected events—from illness to accidents to economic downturns—can unravel even the most carefully constructed financial plans. This is where insurance and financial safeguards come into play, serving as the foundation of long-term stability and peace of mind.

Private health insurance is another critical component, particularly in countries like the UK, where it supplements the National Health Service (NHS). While the NHS provides excellent care and is funded through taxation, it often faces challenges such as long waiting times for elective procedures and limited access to certain specialists or treatments. Private health insurance addresses these gaps by offering faster access to care, shorter waiting times, and a broader choice of providers and treatments. This can be especially valuable for individuals with specific medical needs, chronic conditions requiring ongoing attention, or those who want more flexibility and convenience in managing their healthcare.

The cost of private health insurance varies significantly depending on factors such as age, medical history, and coverage level. For instance, a basic policy for a young, healthy individual might start at around £50-£100 per month, while comprehensive plans for older individuals or those with pre-existing conditions can exceed £200-£300 per month. These costs are in stark contrast to the NHS, where care is free at the point of delivery and funded through National Insurance contributions. However, the added convenience and enhanced options provided by private insurance often justify the expense for those who can afford it.

When comparing private health insurance to NHS care, it's important to consider your specific needs. For example, if you require routine access to specialists or are considering elective procedures that might face long NHS waiting lists, private insurance can significantly reduce delays. Conversely, for emergency or critical care, the NHS remains one of the best systems globally, providing life-saving treatment without the need for insurance or upfront costs.

Selecting the right private health insurance plan involves balancing cost, coverage, and the unique healthcare needs of you and your family. It's also worth noting that not everyone benefits equally from private insurance. For those who are young, healthy, and satisfied with NHS services, private health insurance might not be necessary. However, for families, individuals with specific medical concerns, or those seeking faster access to treatment, it can provide invaluable peace of mind and a more tailored healthcare experience.

Home insurance is a foundational safeguard for protecting your physical assets. Whether you own or rent, ensuring your property and belongings are covered against theft, natural disasters, or accidental damage is essential. For homeowners, comprehensive policies often include liability protection, covering incidents where someone is injured on your property. Renters, too, benefit from content insurance, which shields personal belongings from unforeseen circumstances, reinforcing the idea that safeguarding is not exclusive to property owners.

Life insurance is often the first step in securing your financial legacy, but it is just one of many tools available for safeguarding your wealth. Life insurance provides essential protection for your loved ones, ensuring that they can maintain their standard of living, pay off debts, and cover future expenses in your absence. For families, this safety net can mean the difference between financial security and economic hardship, especially during emotionally challenging times. Beyond the immediate financial relief, life insurance offers a sense of stability and continuity, allowing your family to focus on rebuilding their lives without the added stress of financial strain.

Travel insurance is another often overlooked but vital safeguard, especially for frequent travelers or those embarking on significant trips. It provides a wide range of protections, including coverage for medical emergencies abroad, trip cancellations, lost or delayed luggage, and even flight interruptions. Without this protection, the financial burden of an unexpected incident can be immense, turning what should be a relaxing or productive journey into a stressful and costly ordeal.

One of the most critical aspects of travel insurance is its medical coverage, which can be a lifesaver in countries where healthcare costs are exorbitant. For instance, a simple hospital visit in the United States can cost thousands of dollars, while emergency evacuations from remote areas or cruise ships can run into tens of thousands. Comprehensive travel insurance not only covers these costs but often includes assistance services, such as arranging medical transport or finding local healthcare providers, ensuring you receive the care you need promptly.

Travel insurance also protects against non-medical disruptions. If your trip is canceled or curtailed due to unforeseen circumstances such as illness, natural disasters, or political instability, the policy can reimburse non-refundable expenses like flights, hotels, or tours. Additionally, coverage for lost or delayed luggage provides financial relief to replace essential items, ensuring that a logistical hiccup doesn't derail your plans entirely.

When choosing travel insurance, it's important to evaluate policies carefully. Some plans offer comprehensive coverage, including adventure sports or activities, while others may exclude these higher-risk pursuits. Frequent travelers might benefit from annual multi-trip policies, which provide coverage for multiple journeys within a year and often prove more cost-effective than single-trip plans.

However, not all travel insurance is created equal. Some policies may have high deductibles, limited coverage caps, or exclusions that render them less effective. Reviewing the fine print and comparing policies ensures you choose one that aligns with your needs and travel style, providing robust protection without unnecessary add-ons.

That said, not all insurance products provide equal value, and some may be unnecessary depending on your circumstances. Payment protection insurance (PPI), for instance, is often redundant if you already have comprehensive income protection or a well-established emergency savings fund. Many PPI policies have historically been criticized for their limited scope and high costs, making them an inefficient choice for most individuals.

Similarly, gadget insurance might seem appealing, especially for those who rely heavily on electronics like smartphones or laptops, but it often duplicates coverage already provided through home insurance policies or extended warranties offered by manufacturers. For instance, a homeowner's policy might already cover accidental damage or theft of personal electronics, rendering additional gadget insurance redundant. It's essential to review the terms of your existing coverage before purchasing such policies.

Another example of potentially unnecessary insurance is accidental death and dismemberment (AD&D) insurance, which overlaps with coverage typically found in comprehensive life or health insurance policies. While AD&D policies provide payouts for specific scenarios, their narrow scope means they rarely offer the broad protection needed to address a family's financial security.

Even extended warranties for appliances or vehicles can fall into this category of questionable value. While they promise peace of mind, the cost of these warranties often exceeds the average repair expenses, especially for reliable brands or newer models still under the manufacturer's warranty. Assessing the reliability of the product and the likelihood of needing repairs is crucial before purchasing such add-ons.

The key to making informed decisions about insurance is understanding your actual risks and evaluating your existing protections. Avoid over-insuring by focusing on policies that address significant vulnerabilities in your financial plan. This approach ensures your resources are allocated efficiently, allowing you to prioritize robust, essential protections like life, health, and income protection insurance over redundant or narrowly focused products. By tailoring your coverage to your needs, you can strike a balance between preparedness and cost-effectiveness.

Choosing the right type of policy is critical and should align with your financial goals and family's needs. Term life insurance offers affordable coverage for a fixed period, making it an excellent choice for young families or individuals with temporary financial obligations like a mortgage or children's education expenses. Whole life insurance, on the other hand, provides lifetime coverage and includes a cash value component that grows over time. This makes it a more expensive option but one that can serve as both a protective measure and a financial asset. Universal life insurance combines elements of both term and whole life policies, offering flexibility in premiums and coverage while also building cash value. However, it requires careful management to ensure it meets your long-term goals.

For example, a young couple with a mortgage and two small children might opt for a term policy covering 20 years, ensuring that the mortgage is paid off and the children's education funded in the event of an untimely death. Meanwhile, an older individual nearing retirement might choose a whole life policy to leave a financial legacy or cover estate taxes. These decisions depend on factors such as age, income, debt levels, and long-term aspirations, highlighting the importance of tailoring coverage to fit your unique circumstances.

Income protection insurance is another vital safeguard, particularly for individuals whose livelihoods depend on a steady paycheck. This type of policy provides a portion of your income if you're unable to work due to illness or injury. It ensures that your financial obligations, such as mortgage payments or daily expenses, can still be met, preventing the need to dip into savings or sell off investments prematurely. Critical illness insurance, which provides a lump sum upon diagnosis of a serious condition, complements income protection by covering additional costs, such as medical treatments or home modifications.

Beyond individual policies, safeguarding your wealth also involves a comprehensive approach to protecting physical and financial assets. Home insurance acts as a cornerstone, providing coverage against damage, theft, and unforeseen natural disasters. This ensures that your property and belongings are shielded, offering financial relief during difficult times and helping you rebuild without incurring significant out-of-pocket expenses. For renters, content insurance offers similar protection for personal belongings, emphasizing that home coverage isn't limited to property owners.

Health insurance is equally vital, ensuring access to necessary medical care without the risk of catastrophic costs. In countries with universal healthcare, private health insurance can still play an important role by providing expedited access to specialists, elective procedures, and a broader range of treatments. For those in countries without universal healthcare, health insurance becomes an indispensable safeguard against exorbitant medical bills that could derail even the most carefully laid financial plans.

For business owners, the stakes are even higher when it comes to safeguarding their financial stability. Liability insurance serves as a critical safeguard, protecting against claims arising from accidents, injuries, or negligence that could otherwise pose existential threats to the enterprise. For example, a customer slipping on wet floors in a store could result in a costly legal battle, which liability insurance can help mitigate. Without such coverage, businesses might face overwhelming financial burdens that jeopardize their operations and long-term survival.

Professional indemnity insurance extends this safety net by covering claims of malpractice, errors, or omissions, particularly for service-based industries. For instance, an architect accused of design flaws in a building project could face significant legal and reputational risks. Professional indemnity insurance not only provides financial protection but also reinforces trust and credibility with clients and stakeholders, positioning the business as reliable and accountable.

For landlords, the landscape of risk is distinct yet equally pressing. Specific insurance policies cater to the unique challenges of property rental, such as loss of rental income due to tenant default or property damage caused by unforeseen events like fires or floods. These policies ensure that rental properties remain viable investments even in the face of disruptions. Moreover, landlord liability insurance provides coverage if a tenant or visitor is injured on the property, safeguarding against potential lawsuits.

In addition to these essential protections, businesses and landlords must consider the broader implications of insurance on their long-term growth. Comprehensive coverage not only shields against immediate risks but also enhances the enterprise's resilience, enabling it to navigate challenges without compromising financial stability. By proactively addressing these vulnerabilities, business owners and landlords can focus on growth and innovation with confidence, knowing that their foundational assets are secure.

Ultimately, securing your wealth isn't just about preparing for the worst; it's about creating a foundation for continued growth and opportunity. With the right protections in place, you can pursue your financial goals with confidence, knowing that you and your loved ones are protected from life's uncertainties.

Generational Wealth: Building a Legacy

Building generational wealth is about more than amassing assets; it's about creating a sustainable foundation that supports your family for decades to come. This process requires a thoughtful combination of financial education, strategic investments, and meticulous planning to ensure your wealth is preserved, grows over time, and is transferred efficiently to future generations.

At its core, generational wealth isn't just about money—it's about values and the knowledge passed down through the generations. By instilling financial literacy and teaching stewardship, you equip your family with the tools they need not only to inherit wealth but to expand it responsibly. Conversations about money should start early, laying the foundation for financial competence that grows as children mature. Teaching young family members the basics of budgeting, saving, and understanding the value of money helps them develop the discipline and habits necessary to manage finances effectively.

As children grow, these lessons should evolve to include more complex topics such as investing, asset diversification, and the importance of long-term financial planning. For instance, introducing teenagers to the basics of compound interest and the benefits of starting an investment portfolio early can set them on a path to financial independence. For adult family members, discussions might center around more advanced concepts like tax strategies, estate planning, or entrepreneurship. By making financial literacy an ongoing dialogue, you ensure that every generation is well-prepared to handle and grow the family's wealth.

Beyond financial skills, instilling a sense of stewardship is essential. Wealthy families often stress the importance of seeing themselves as caretakers of their resources rather than mere beneficiaries. This mindset fosters a long-term perspective, encouraging each generation to consider how their actions today will impact future family members. This could involve teaching the importance of preserving assets, reinvesting profits, and making decisions that align with the family's core values.

Storytelling plays a significant role in reinforcing these lessons. Sharing the origins of the family's wealth—whether it was built through entrepreneurship, hard work, or smart investments—helps instill pride and a sense of responsibility. Stories of past challenges and successes provide context, reminding younger generations that wealth is not simply a result of luck but a culmination of effort, strategy, and resilience. These narratives can be powerful motivators, encouraging family members to honor and build upon the legacy they inherit.

Incorporating shared experiences, such as working on a family business or participating in philanthropic projects, can also strengthen the bond between family members while reinforcing the values that underpin their wealth. These activities not only teach practical skills but also cultivate a sense of purpose and collaboration, ensuring that the family's wealth serves as a unifying force rather than a source of division.

Ultimately, while money provides the means, it is the knowledge, values, and shared vision that sustain generational wealth. Together, they form the foundation of a lasting legacy that empowers each generation to build upon the successes of the past while navigating the challenges of the future.

Strategic Investments: Building a Solid Foundation

Strategic investments are the bedrock of generational wealth. Diversifying your portfolio across assets like stocks, real estate, and bonds ensures both stability and growth potential. Real estate, in particular, offers a unique advantage. Beyond providing tangible value, real estate investments often generate passive income through rental properties or appreciation over time. A carefully managed portfolio of real estate can create a steady stream of income that supports multiple generations.

Business ventures also play a vital role in creating wealth. Starting a family business or investing in long-term projects allows for wealth generation while fostering shared purpose and collaboration among family members. Involving your children in the management and growth of a family business not only teaches valuable entrepreneurial skills but also strengthens their sense of responsibility and connection to the legacy.

Investment vehicles such as index funds, mutual funds, and exchange-traded funds (ETFs) provide accessible ways to grow wealth consistently. These instruments often balance risk and reward effectively, making them ideal for long-term strategies. Additionally, considering alternative investments, such as art, precious metals, or even venture capital, can diversify your portfolio further and offer unique opportunities for growth.

Wills, Trusts, and Estate Planning: Protecting Your Legacy

Proper estate planning ensures that your wealth is distributed according to your wishes while minimizing unnecessary taxes and legal challenges. A will is the cornerstone of any estate plan, specifying how your assets should be allocated and who will be responsible for executing your wishes. Without a will, your estate may be subjected to lengthy probate processes, leaving your family vulnerable to disputes, delays, and potentially significant legal expenses. This can create unnecessary stress for your loved ones during an already challenging time.

When it comes to passing down property, careful planning is particularly important. Real estate often represents one of the most valuable assets in an estate, and transferring it efficiently can prevent both emotional and financial complications. For example, placing property in a trust can allow for a seamless transfer to heirs, bypassing probate entirely. Trusts not only expedite the process but also provide privacy, as they are not subject to public record like wills. Furthermore, they can help reduce inheritance tax liabilities by excluding the property from the taxable estate, provided the trust is set up properly and in compliance with relevant laws.

In the UK, inheritance tax planning is crucial for property owners, as properties can easily push estates above the tax-free threshold of £325,000. Gifting property during your lifetime is one strategy to mitigate this. If the gift is made at least seven years before death, it may not be subject to inheritance tax, though proper legal advice is essential to navigate potential pitfalls, such as capital gains tax. Another approach is utilizing the residence nil-rate band, an additional allowance that can reduce the tax burden when passing down the family home to direct descendants, such as children or grandchildren.

In the United States, property inheritance can similarly be optimized through strategic planning. The federal estate tax exemption, currently over $12 million per individual, provides significant leeway for high-value estates. However, state-level estate or inheritance taxes may still apply. Establishing irrevocable trusts, leveraging the step-up in basis rules for inherited properties, or gifting portions of the property over time can help minimize tax liabilities while ensuring the property remains within the family.

Effective estate planning also involves clear communication with heirs about their roles and responsibilities. Discussing your intentions openly helps prevent misunderstandings or conflicts, ensuring a smoother transition. By combining legal tools like wills and trusts with proactive tax strategies and transparent family dialogue, you can ensure that your property and legacy are preserved for future generations.

Trusts provide even greater flexibility and protection, making them an indispensable tool in estate planning. By placing assets in a trust, you can bypass probate entirely, ensuring a smoother, faster, and more private transfer of wealth. The probate process, while necessary in many cases, can be lengthy and public, subjecting your family to potential delays and scrutiny. Trusts shield your assets from these challenges, allowing your wealth to be distributed according to your wishes without external interference.

Trusts can be tailored to meet highly specific needs, offering unparalleled versatility. For example, a trust can be established to provide for minor children, ensuring they have financial support until they reach adulthood. These funds can be allocated for educational expenses, healthcare, or general living costs. Additionally, trusts are invaluable for safeguarding assets for individuals with disabilities, ensuring their needs are met without jeopardizing eligibility for government assistance programs.

Conditional trusts are another innovative solution, allowing you to set parameters for how and when beneficiaries receive funds. For instance, you might specify that funds be distributed only when a beneficiary reaches a certain age, completes a degree, or demonstrates financial responsibility. These conditions ensure that your wealth is not only preserved but also used in ways that align with your values and intentions.

Moreover, trusts can protect your assets from creditors and legal disputes, adding an extra layer of security to your legacy. By establishing an irrevocable trust, for example, assets are no longer considered part of your personal estate, shielding them from claims in the event of financial or legal challenges. This protection ensures that your wealth remains intact for your intended beneficiaries.

In today's increasingly complex financial landscape, trusts are not just a tool for the wealthy—they are a practical solution for anyone seeking to preserve and manage their assets effectively. By leveraging the flexibility and security that trusts offer, you create a robust framework for wealth transfer that prioritizes the well-being and stability of your loved ones for generations to come.

Life insurance can also play a pivotal role in estate planning. It provides liquidity to cover expenses such as estate taxes, debts, or funeral costs, preventing the need to sell valuable assets during difficult times. Additionally, charitable giving through family foundations or donor-advised funds can create a lasting impact while offering significant tax advantages, aligning your legacy with your values and passions.

Minimizing Tax Burden: A Critical Strategy

One of the most significant threats to generational wealth is taxation. Careful planning is required to minimize inheritance taxes, capital gains taxes, and other levies that can erode your estate. For example, in the UK, the inheritance tax threshold is currently set at £325,000, with anything above this amount subject to a 40% tax rate. Strategies such as gifting assets during your lifetime, using trust structures, or leveraging annual exemptions can reduce this burden significantly.

To address these challenges, families often turn to a variety of strategies designed to reduce their tax liabilities. One highly effective approach is gifting assets during one's lifetime. Gifts made more than seven years prior to death are exempt from inheritance tax, allowing families to transfer wealth efficiently over time. Spreading these gifts across multiple years and taking advantage of annual exemptions, such as the £3,000 annual gift allowance, can ensure that transfers remain within tax-free limits. However, families must also consider potential capital gains tax liabilities that may arise from transferring certain assets, like property or shares.

The residence nil-rate band (RNRB) provides additional relief for families passing down their primary residence to direct descendants. Currently, the RNRB allows an additional £175,000 per individual, potentially increasing the total tax-free threshold for married couples or civil partners to £1 million when combined with the standard nil-rate band. Proper estate planning is essential to ensure eligibility for this relief, particularly for high-value estates where tapering thresholds may apply, potentially reducing the RNRB for estates exceeding £2 million.

Trusts are another indispensable tool in minimizing taxes and protecting wealth. By placing assets into a trust, families can remove them from the taxable estate, thereby reducing IHT liabilities. Trusts also offer flexibility and control, allowing individuals to dictate how and when assets are distributed. For instance, a discretionary trust can allocate income or capital to beneficiaries as needed, providing both protection and adaptability. Trusts also provide privacy by avoiding the public probate process, shielding sensitive financial details from scrutiny.

Charitable giving is another powerful strategy for reducing tax burdens while aligning wealth with personal values. Donations to qualified charities reduce the taxable portion of the estate and can lower the IHT rate to 36% if at least 10% of the net estate is donated. This approach not only minimizes tax liabilities but also reinforces the values of generosity and social responsibility within the family, creating a legacy that extends beyond financial wealth.

Establishing donor-advised funds or family foundations offers a structured way to make an impact, enabling families to support causes they care about deeply while maintaining control over how funds are distributed over time. These philanthropic vehicles allow families to set specific goals for their charitable giving, such as funding educational programs, supporting medical research, or contributing to environmental sustainability initiatives. They also provide an opportunity to involve multiple generations in the decision-making process, fostering collaboration and shared purpose among family members.

Philanthropy can also serve as an educational tool, teaching younger generations about the importance of giving back and managing resources responsibly. For example, families can create advisory boards for their foundations, inviting children or grandchildren to participate and gain hands-on experience in governance, budgeting, and impact measurement. These experiences not only build financial acumen but also instill values of empathy and community engagement, ensuring that the family's commitment to social good endures.

Moreover, large charitable contributions can strengthen relationships with communities and enhance the family's reputation. Endowing scholarships, funding local initiatives, or supporting disaster relief efforts can leave a visible and lasting impact, showcasing the family's dedication to societal well-being. This positive public perception can open doors to new opportunities and partnerships, further enhancing the family's influence and reach.

For high-net-worth families, charitable giving also presents an opportunity to align wealth management with tax optimization strategies. Contributions can be made in various forms, including cash donations, appreciated securities, or even real estate. Donating appreciated assets provides dual benefits: the donor avoids capital gains tax on the asset's growth while receiving a tax deduction for its fair market value. These strategies maximize the financial and social impact of the family's wealth while ensuring tax efficiency.

By integrating charitable giving into a comprehensive estate plan, families can ensure their wealth serves both their heirs and the broader community. This dual focus creates a balanced approach to legacy building, where financial resources not only secure the future for descendants but also contribute meaningfully to the world. In doing so, families establish a legacy that is remembered not just for the assets passed down but for the positive change they inspired.

In addition to these strategies, retaining highly appreciated assets until death can leverage the step-up in basis rules, significantly reducing capital gains tax liabilities for heirs. When an asset is inherited, its value is "stepped up" to its current market value, meaning heirs only pay taxes on gains made after the inheritance. This approach underscores the importance of retaining certain assets within the estate to optimize tax outcomes.

Ultimately, effective tax planning requires not just legal tools but also open communication within families. Discussing these strategies openly helps manage expectations, ensures that everyone understands the purpose and value of the plan, and fosters a sense of shared responsibility. By combining these elements, families can preserve their wealth while creating a lasting legacy that supports future generations.

In the United States, similar strategies apply, but they often require even more nuanced planning due to the complexity of federal and state tax laws. The federal estate tax exemption, currently over $12 million per individual as of 2024, provides significant leeway for high-net-worth individuals. However, this threshold is not permanent and may change with shifts in government policy. For families with estates exceeding this amount, strategic planning is essential to minimize tax liabilities and ensure that wealth remains intact for future generations.

One of the most effective strategies involves gifting assets during one's lifetime. By gradually transferring portions of wealth to heirs through the annual gift tax exclusion—which allows individuals to gift up to $17,000 per recipient tax-free as of 2024—families can significantly reduce the size of their taxable estate. Over time, these incremental transfers can add up, preserving wealth while minimizing exposure to estate taxes.

Charitable donations also play a dual role in preserving wealth and creating a meaningful legacy. By donating to qualified charities, families can receive substantial tax deductions, reducing the taxable portion of their estate. Establishing donor-advised funds or family foundations further allows families to align their charitable giving with their values while reaping tax benefits.

Irrevocable trusts offer another powerful tool for minimizing taxes and ensuring the smooth transfer of assets. These trusts remove assets from the taxable estate, shielding them from both estate taxes and potential creditors. For example, a grantor-retained annuity trust (GRAT) allows individuals to transfer appreciating assets to heirs with minimal tax implications. Similarly, generation-skipping trusts can help families transfer wealth directly to grandchildren, bypassing one layer of estate tax entirely.

Additionally, leveraging the step-up in basis rules for inherited properties can significantly reduce capital gains taxes for heirs. When a property is inherited, its value is typically "stepped up" to the current market value, meaning heirs only pay taxes on gains made after the inheritance. This provision underscores the importance of retaining certain highly appreciated assets within the estate until death.

By combining these techniques, families can not only preserve their wealth but also ensure that it is distributed according to their wishes, supporting both immediate heirs and future generations. Open communication with heirs about these strategies is equally important, as it helps manage expectations and ensures everyone understands the purpose and value of the plans in place.

The Human Element: Values and Knowledge

Beyond financial tools and strategies, the human element is what truly defines generational wealth. Building a legacy isn't just about passing down assets; it's about passing down knowledge, values, and a sense of purpose. Wealthy families often maintain their financial success across generations not solely because of the money but because of the knowledge and principles they instill in their descendants. By fostering a culture of education and stewardship, they equip future generations with the tools and mindset needed to preserve and grow wealth responsibly.

Family meetings can be an excellent forum to discuss goals, review financial plans, and ensure that everyone is aligned. These gatherings are not merely administrative; they are opportunities to strengthen family bonds and create a shared vision for the future. During these discussions, younger family members can be introduced to the intricacies of managing wealth, such as budgeting, investing, and philanthropy, ensuring they understand the responsibilities and privileges that come with financial success.

In addition to formal education, storytelling plays a powerful role in passing down values. Sharing the origins of the family's wealth—

whether it was built through hard work, entrepreneurship, or savvy investments—instills a sense of pride and continuity. For example, recounting stories of how a family business was started or how a grandparent overcame adversity to create opportunities can inspire younger generations to appreciate and respect the legacy they inherit. These narratives emphasize that wealth is not simply a result of luck but a culmination of effort, resilience, and foresight.

Moreover, wealthy families often prioritize teaching the importance of giving back. By engaging in philanthropic efforts together, they reinforce values of compassion and responsibility. This could involve creating family foundations, participating in community service, or establishing scholarships, which not only benefit society but also unite the family around a common purpose.

Passing down knowledge is as critical as transferring financial assets. While money provides the means, education provides the method. Together, they form the foundation of a lasting legacy that empowers each generation to build upon the successes of the past.

Storytelling can play a powerful role in this process. Sharing the origins of the family's wealth—whether it was built through hard work, entrepreneurship, or savvy investments—helps instill a sense of pride and continuity. By emphasizing the values that underpin the family's success, you create a culture of stewardship that prioritizes long-term thinking over short-term gratification.

Sustaining Prosperity Across Generations

Building generational wealth requires foresight, discipline, and a commitment to nurturing the values and knowledge that will sustain your family's prosperity for years to come. It's not just about creating wealth but ensuring that it empowers future generations to thrive and adapt to an ever-changing world. Wealth, when paired with wisdom, becomes a powerful tool for stability and growth, allowing families to not only weather challenges but also seize opportunities with confidence.

A critical part of this process is instilling the understanding that wealth comes with responsibility. Each generation must embrace the role of steward, recognizing that the decisions they make today will shape the future for those who follow. This sense of accountability encourages thoughtful decision-making and ensures that wealth is not squandered but leveraged to create meaningful impact.

Passing down property, businesses, and investments is part of the puzzle, but the intangible elements—values, resilience, and shared purpose—are what truly ensure longevity. Families that emphasize the importance of unity and collaboration often find greater success in preserving their wealth across generations. Regular communication, family councils, and shared projects can strengthen these bonds, creating a cohesive vision that guides financial and personal decisions alike.

Ultimately, building generational wealth is a marathon, not a sprint. It requires patience, adaptability, and a willingness to learn from both successes and setbacks. Through education, strategic investments, and comprehensive planning, you lay the groundwork for a legacy that endures. By combining these elements with a focus on shared purpose, adaptability, and a commitment to growth, your family can navigate challenges and seize opportunities, securing a brighter future for all who follow. The true measure of success lies not only in the assets passed down but in the values and opportunities you provide for the generations to come.

Part 7: Beyond Financial Success

Legacy and Giving Back: Leaving More Than Breadcrumbs

Building generational wealth and giving back to your community. Building generational wealth is a significant achievement, but true success extends beyond financial prosperity. It lies in the ability to leave a lasting impact on your community and the world around you. By prioritizing giving back and establishing a meaningful legacy, you can create a ripple effect that benefits future generations far beyond your immediate family.

Legacy is about more than the money or assets you pass down; it encompasses your values, vision, and the ways in which your life has positively influenced others. It is the emotional, moral, and philosophical footprint you leave behind. A well-rounded legacy includes contributions to your family, community, and society. Reflecting on your personal values and long-term goals is an essential first step in crafting this legacy. Ask yourself: What do you want to be remembered for? How can your resources, knowledge, and influence best support the causes and people that matter most to you?

For many, creating a legacy involves blending financial planning with philanthropy. This can take various forms, from funding community programs to establishing scholarships, supporting nonprofit organizations, or contributing to global causes. Thoughtful giving not only amplifies the impact of your wealth but also ensures that your contributions reflect your deepest values and priorities. For example, creating an endowment for a local school can help support education for decades, while funding a clean water project might improve health outcomes for entire communities.

Giving back isn't just about charity; it's about empowerment, sustainability, and creating a legacy of meaningful change. When you invest in your community, you don't just address immediate needs—you help build the foundations for long-term success and resilience. Whether it's funding education initiatives, supporting healthcare programs, or investing in sustainable development, your contributions have the potential to tackle systemic issues, bridge gaps, and create enduring solutions.

Endowing a scholarship fund for underprivileged students, for example, can do more than just provide financial support; it can offer hope, open doors, and fundamentally transform life trajectories. By giving these students access to education, you help them break free from entrenched cycles of poverty and disadvantage, empowering them to pursue careers, aspirations, and opportunities that benefit not only their own families but also their broader communities. These scholarships create a pathway to success that would otherwise remain inaccessible for many, opening doors to industries, professions, and possibilities that were once out of reach.

Education is one of the most powerful tools for long-term societal change. It is a multiplier, creating ripples of positive impact that extend across generations and reshape communities. A single scholarship can spark a chain reaction: the recipient gains the skills and confidence to achieve their goals, and in turn, they inspire others to follow suit. These graduates often return to their communities as leaders, role models, and advocates for progress, further magnifying the effects of your generosity.

Moreover, scholarships contribute to breaking systemic barriers by leveling the playing field for those who face economic or social obstacles. They enable students to focus on their studies without the added burden of financial stress, fostering an environment where they can fully realize their potential. The knowledge and skills they acquire through education have a compounding effect, enhancing not only their personal lives but also the economic and cultural vitality of their communities. By investing in their futures, you are indirectly investing in stronger, more equitable societies.

The benefits of these scholarships also extend into the workforce. Providing access to higher education creates a pool of skilled and talented individuals who drive innovation, contribute to local and global economies, and tackle pressing challenges. These students are more likely to develop solutions for their communities, close gaps in representation within various industries, and advocate for inclusive practices, ensuring a more just and balanced future.

Your contributions can be the catalyst that sets these transformations in motion, offering opportunities that multiply and evolve over time. By endowing scholarships, you are not only changing individual lives but also shaping the trajectory of entire generations and communities, creating a legacy of empowerment and progress.

Similarly, supporting healthcare initiatives improves not just individual well-being but also the overall health of a region. Access to quality healthcare reduces disparities, ensures healthier lives, and fosters productivity and resilience within the community. Contributions to healthcare programs can provide life-saving medical equipment, fund preventative care initiatives, or expand access to underserved populations. These actions don't just solve problems in the moment—they lay the groundwork for a stronger, healthier society that can thrive for years to come.

Investing in sustainable development adds another vital dimension to giving back. Renewable energy projects, environmental conservation efforts, and sustainable agriculture initiatives address some of the most pressing challenges of our time while ensuring that resources are preserved for future generations. For instance, funding solar energy programs in remote areas not only provides immediate access to power but also reduces dependency on nonrenewable resources, promoting environmental stewardship. Supporting reforestation projects or marine conservation efforts safeguards ecosystems that countless species, including humans, depend on. These contributions tackle global challenges while leaving a lasting legacy of environmental care and responsibility.

By prioritizing these types of investments, you transform the act of giving into a force for systemic change. Your generosity becomes a powerful tool for empowerment, addressing root causes of inequality and fostering a culture of shared progress. Each initiative you support contributes to a mosaic of positive transformation, creating a legacy that not only uplifts individuals but strengthens communities and protects the planet for future generations.

Effective philanthropy requires careful planning, intentionality, and a clear vision of the impact you want to achieve. Establishing a family foundation or donor-advised fund can provide the structure needed to manage charitable giving strategically, ensuring that your resources are used in alignment with your mission and values. These vehicles allow you to allocate funds thoughtfully and ensure that donations are directed to causes that truly matter to you. By setting up a family foundation, you not only create a centralized platform for your giving but also foster collaboration and engagement among multiple generations. Involving younger family members in the decision-making process instills a sense of responsibility and ensures that your legacy of generosity endures.

Donor-advised funds offer unparalleled flexibility, enabling you to contribute various assets, including cash, stocks, or real estate, while retaining the ability to recommend grants to charities over time. This flexibility allows you to adapt your giving to evolving priorities and societal needs, ensuring that your philanthropy remains relevant and impactful. Additionally, these tools provide significant tax advantages, such as immediate deductions for contributions and the ability to grow charitable assets tax-free, which can maximize the reach of your generosity.

Beyond the logistical benefits, the act of giving back when you have accumulated significant wealth has profound personal and societal implications. Financial success opens the door to transformative opportunities—not just for your family but for entire communities. By leveraging your resources to address systemic issues, you can create lasting change that extends far beyond monetary contributions. Giving back also fosters a deeper sense of purpose and fulfillment, allowing you to connect your success with meaningful outcomes. It transforms wealth from a personal achievement into a tool for empowerment and progress.

Engaging in strategic philanthropy also enhances your legacy, demonstrating that financial success is most meaningful when shared. Your actions inspire others—family, peers, and even strangers—to recognize the power of giving and to consider how they, too, can contribute to the greater good. Ultimately, effective philanthropy ensures that your wealth is not just a reflection of what you have achieved, but a testament to the positive change you have created in the world.

Passing down the value of giving is as important as passing down financial wealth. Involving children or grandchildren in philanthropic activities helps them understand the importance of using their resources to benefit others. Family meetings can serve as a platform for discussing charitable goals and identifying causes that resonate with everyone. This not only fosters unity but also empowers younger generations to carry forward the family's legacy of generosity. Encouraging hands-on involvement, such as volunteering or participating in community projects, deepens their connection to the causes they support. These experiences provide valuable lessons in empathy, leadership, and collaboration, shaping their character and ensuring that the legacy of giving endures.

While giving back is vital, it is equally important to strike a balance between philanthropy and ensuring the long-term security of your family. Comprehensive financial planning allows you to allocate resources effectively, ensuring that your wealth supports both your heirs and your philanthropic endeavors. Establishing clear boundaries and priorities ensures that your giving aligns with your overall financial goals. For instance, setting aside a portion of your estate specifically for charitable purposes—whether through a trust, endowment, or foundation—provides clarity and ensures that your legacy is preserved. At the same time, maintaining investments and assets for family use ensures that descendants are well-provided for, allowing them to continue the cycle of growth and giving.

A legacy isn't static; it evolves over time and adapts to the shifting needs and opportunities within your community and family. As the world changes, so too must the approaches and priorities of your philanthropic efforts. Regularly reassessing your goals allows you to respond effectively to emerging societal challenges, ensuring that your contributions remain impactful and meaningful in an ever-evolving landscape. This process of reflection and adaptation strengthens your legacy, allowing it to stay relevant and aligned with both your values and the needs of the moment.

For example, as new technologies emerge, they can create opportunities for innovative solutions that address long-standing issues in novel ways. Supporting initiatives that leverage technology—such as using artificial intelligence for healthcare diagnostics in underserved regions or funding online education platforms for remote learning—can dramatically expand the reach and effectiveness of your contributions.

Similarly, as social issues become more pressing, directing resources toward underserved communities or urgent causes can help mitigate disparities and bring about meaningful progress where it is most needed.

Staying engaged with the issues you care about ensures that your legacy continues to resonate with the changing priorities of society. This engagement might involve building relationships with thought leaders in your areas of interest, attending conferences, or staying informed about trends in philanthropy and social innovation. By maintaining this active involvement, you amplify not only the relevance of your legacy but also its reach, inspiring others to join you in creating positive change. This constant evolution ensures that your contributions remain a powerful force for good, capable of making a lasting difference no matter how the world transforms around them.

By staying proactive, you inspire others to carry the torch. Your actions serve as a blueprint for family members, peers, and community leaders, demonstrating the power of sustained commitment to giving back. Whether through direct contributions or by fostering collaboration with others, your influence can extend far beyond individual efforts, creating a collective movement toward positive change. Beyond the direct impact of your contributions, the example you set can transform the mindset of those around you. By showing consistent dedication to giving back, you encourage others to adopt similar values of generosity and responsibility. This ripple effect has the potential to inspire a culture of giving that transcends your immediate influence, creating a far-reaching legacy of kindness and impact.

In this way, your legacy becomes not only a means of personal fulfillment but also a catalyst for widespread improvement. It exemplifies the idea that true success isn't measured solely by wealth accumulated but by the enduring positive changes initiated and sustained through your actions and values.

Building a legacy is about creating something enduring that transcends your lifetime. It's about combining financial success with purpose, ensuring that your wealth leaves a mark not just on your family but also on the world. True legacy-building involves intentional actions that reflect your core values, ensuring your resources support meaningful change and uplift those around you.

Creating a legacy requires more than just financial assets; it involves shaping a narrative of impact, purpose, and enduring influence. Generosity is not only about giving away wealth but about fostering opportunities, strengthening communities, and instilling values that transcend individual efforts. By prioritizing generosity, you lay the groundwork for a transformative influence that inspires others, encouraging them to aspire to a higher purpose. This generosity acts as a powerful catalyst, spreading opportunity and fostering a culture of empowerment within communities.

Involving future generations in this vision ensures that your values endure, becoming deeply embedded in the lives and decisions of those who follow. When younger family members are included in conversations about the family's legacy, they develop a greater sense of responsibility and connection to the broader impact of their inheritance. This involvement not only preserves your principles but also equips the next generation to continue building on your efforts, ensuring that the legacy of generosity expands and thrives over time.

Furthermore, creating a legacy rooted in generosity allows for the creation of structures that address systemic challenges. These efforts can range from funding educational programs that uplift underserved communities to establishing initiatives that tackle environmental challenges or improve access to healthcare. Each act of giving reverberates through communities, multiplying its impact and fostering resilience among those who benefit from it. Through such deliberate and expansive acts, your legacy becomes a testament to the belief that wealth is most meaningful when used to create a better world.

Strategic planning is crucial to magnify the reach of your legacy. By aligning your philanthropic efforts with carefully chosen causes, you can drive sustainable change and create a ripple effect that extends across multiple generations. Whether it's funding education programs, supporting healthcare initiatives, or investing in global environmental solutions, these contributions become enduring testaments to your dedication and foresight.

Legacy-building is also about adaptability. As the world evolves, so too must your vision and approach to making a difference. The causes and communities you care about may face shifting challenges, and your ability to recalibrate your efforts ensures that your contributions remain relevant and impactful over time. This adaptability is a cornerstone of effective legacy-building, allowing your values and goals to resonate even in changing circumstances.

Regularly reassessing your philanthropic goals ensures that they align with the most pressing societal needs. For example, advancements in technology might open new avenues to address long-standing problems, such as using artificial intelligence to improve access to education or healthcare in underserved regions. Supporting these innovative solutions not only expands the reach of your contributions but also maximizes their effectiveness, ensuring that your legacy evolves alongside societal progress.

Moreover, staying connected to the causes you care about fosters deeper engagement and amplifies the impact of your efforts. This might involve participating in community initiatives, collaborating with experts, or attending forums and conferences to stay informed about emerging trends. By remaining actively involved, you demonstrate a commitment that inspires others and establishes your contributions as a dynamic force for good.

Adaptability also allows you to seize new opportunities as they arise, whether through investing in groundbreaking research, supporting timely disaster relief efforts, or addressing newly identified gaps in social services. This flexibility ensures that your legacy is not static but a living, evolving testament to your commitment to making a meaningful difference. Ultimately, by embracing change and innovation, you create a legacy that is not only enduring but also deeply attuned to the needs of future generations.

Ultimately, true success lies not only in the wealth you accumulate but in the enduring positive changes you initiate and nurture through your actions. Your legacy is not defined by the assets you leave behind but by the pathways you create for others to thrive. By leaving a clear and intentional roadmap, your life's work becomes a guiding light, inspiring others to continue building on the foundation you established. Instead of merely leaving breadcrumbs, you craft a legacy of lasting significance that reverberates far beyond your lifetime.

Mindset Maintenance: Keeping the Hustle Alive

Maintaining the right mindset is the cornerstone of long-term success, especially when navigating the journey of giving back and building a legacy. It is a continuous process of self-reflection, adaptability, and strategic action. Staying motivated requires consistent reflection on your goals and the impact you are making. Remind yourself regularly of the difference your efforts are creating—whether it's empowering individuals, uplifting communities, or transforming societal structures. These reminders reinforce the significance of your actions and fuel your passion to keep going, even during challenging times.

Adapting to changes is equally essential. The world evolves rapidly, and the causes you care about may shift in priority or require new approaches. This fluidity demands a proactive and open-minded approach to maintain your impact. Embracing flexibility and cultivating a willingness to learn ensures that your efforts remain not only relevant but also increasingly effective as circumstances evolve. Seek out opportunities to engage with thought leaders and experts in your chosen fields, as their insights can provide valuable perspectives and guidance.

Engaging in ongoing education and skill-building is another critical component of adaptability. Attending workshops, seminars, or conferences tailored to your philanthropic interests can broaden your understanding of emerging challenges and potential solutions. These events serve as hubs of innovation and collaboration, where you can connect with thought leaders, industry experts, and like-minded individuals who share your vision for meaningful impact. Engaging in such environments fosters a culture of learning and opens the door to fresh perspectives that can reshape your approach to giving back.

For example, learning about new technologies that address systemic issues, such as AI-powered education platforms or advancements in renewable energy, can revolutionize the way you contribute. AI-powered education platforms can democratize learning, breaking down barriers for underserved communities by providing access to high-quality resources and personalized instruction. Similarly, advancements in renewable energy not only tackle climate challenges but also empower marginalized regions by providing affordable and sustainable power solutions. These innovations exemplify how staying informed about cutting-edge developments can significantly enhance the scope and effectiveness of your philanthropic efforts.

Exploring partnerships with organizations already leading in these areas further amplifies the reach and effectiveness of your initiatives.

Collaborative efforts allow you to pool resources, share expertise, and scale projects to achieve broader, more impactful outcomes. Whether partnering with a nonprofit focused on bridging digital divides or a foundation spearheading clean energy adoption, these alliances can transform isolated contributions into systemic solutions. Partnerships also provide opportunities for co-creating initiatives that align closely with your values, ensuring that your efforts have lasting and deeply rooted benefits. Collaborative ventures also create platforms for innovation, where diverse perspectives come together to solve complex problems more effectively.

In addition, actively participating in these networks can lead to unexpected opportunities for innovation and growth. By engaging in dialogue and exchanging ideas with diverse stakeholders, you might uncover synergies that lead to groundbreaking projects or initiatives. These interactions often foster a collaborative spirit that transcends individual goals, resulting in solutions that are greater than the sum of their parts. For instance, combining the expertise of educational technologists with the logistical capabilities of global NGOs could pave the way for a scalable program that addresses both accessibility and infrastructure gaps. Such a program might leverage advanced technologies, like machine learning or blockchain, to streamline processes, increase transparency, and enhance the reach of educational initiatives. These collaborative ventures ensure that your contributions are not only impactful but also sustainable and forward-thinking, setting the stage for a legacy of transformative change.

Furthermore, active participation in these networks can spark entirely new avenues for action. For example, partnerships with innovators in health technology could lead to mobile healthcare units equipped with telemedicine capabilities, bringing critical services to underserved areas. Similarly, engagement with environmental scientists might result in joint efforts to combat climate change through community-driven renewable energy projects or reforestation programs. The cross-pollination of ideas between different sectors opens doors to initiatives that are innovative, practical, and deeply impactful.

Participating in these networks also allows you to build trust and credibility among a diverse group of stakeholders. This trust becomes a foundation for long-term partnerships, enabling you to tackle larger and more complex challenges together. By aligning with others who share your values, you create a coalition of change-makers, each contributing their expertise and resources toward a shared vision. This collective approach amplifies the reach of your efforts and ensures that the changes you initiate are both enduring and scalable. These networks become incubators for progress, where bold ideas are nurtured, refined, and transformed into actionable strategies that benefit communities on a global scale.

Moreover, embracing change also means being willing to revisit and refine your goals. Periodic self-assessments of your contributions can help you identify areas for improvement and adjust your approach to align with shifting societal needs. It's not just about keeping up with change but actively shaping how you respond to it, ensuring that your legacy remains dynamic and responsive. This might include adopting new technologies, shifting focus to emerging issues, or even reevaluating long-standing strategies to maximize impact. By maintaining this mindset, you reinforce the transformative potential of your efforts while staying ahead of challenges, ultimately creating a larger, more sustained impact.

Celebrating milestones is a critical yet often overlooked part of sustaining momentum. Acknowledge your achievements, both big and small. Whether it's reaching a fundraising goal, witnessing the success of a scholarship recipient, or completing a community project, take the time to reflect on these accomplishments. Celebrations not only provide a sense of fulfillment but also inspire those around you to stay committed to the mission. Use these moments to galvanize your network, share your progress, and invite others to join in the journey. Publicly sharing these milestones can also encourage others to contribute or collaborate, expanding the reach and depth of your impact.

In addition to personal satisfaction, celebrating milestones strengthens your network and builds trust among collaborators and beneficiaries. Recognizing the collective effort behind these achievements reinforces relationships and fosters a sense of shared purpose. It demonstrates transparency and accountability, which are essential for sustaining support and credibility in your philanthropic endeavors.

By staying motivated, adapting to changes, and celebrating milestones, you create a sustainable path forward, one that is not only rewarding but also deeply impactful. This mindset not only strengthens your resolve but also ensures that your legacy-building efforts continue to evolve and thrive, adapting to new challenges and opportunities as they arise. Building a legacy is a dynamic process that requires constant growth, learning, and recalibration. It is through this ongoing effort that you can ensure the longevity and effectiveness of your contributions.

The journey of giving back and creating a legacy is not a linear one; it requires resilience, innovation, and the ability to inspire others along the way. Resilience allows you to navigate setbacks and challenges, transforming obstacles into opportunities for growth. Innovation enables you to find creative solutions to complex problems, ensuring that your initiatives remain relevant and impactful in a rapidly changing world. The ability to inspire others is the glue that binds your efforts to a larger community, encouraging collaboration and collective action that amplifies your impact.

Innovation enables you to find creative solutions to complex problems, ensuring that your initiatives remain relevant and impactful in a rapidly changing world. This creativity often involves thinking outside traditional frameworks and embracing emerging technologies, strategies, or collaborations that can amplify your efforts. For instance, leveraging digital tools to streamline communication, using data-driven approaches to target resources effectively, or partnering with unexpected allies can all enhance the reach and efficiency of your initiatives. Innovation ensures that your legacy is not just preserved but continuously evolves to address new challenges and opportunities.

The ability to inspire others is the glue that binds your efforts to a larger community, encouraging collaboration and collective action that amplifies your impact. Inspiration is a catalyst; it motivates people to contribute, support, and carry forward your mission. By sharing your journey, your challenges, and your triumphs, you create a narrative that resonates deeply, igniting a sense of shared purpose. This collective energy transforms isolated actions into a powerful movement, ensuring that the work you start grows far beyond what you could achieve alone. Inspiration fosters a culture of giving, where your efforts ripple outward, influencing and empowering countless others to join you in making a difference.

Furthermore, leaving an enduring mark on the world involves a commitment to both the present and the future. It means ensuring that your efforts today lay the foundation for sustainable progress and prosperity for generations to come. By cultivating these traits and embedding them in your approach, you transform the act of giving back into a powerful legacy that continues to grow and inspire long after your direct involvement. Your dedication becomes a beacon of hope and a source of motivation for others to carry the torch forward, creating a ripple effect of positive change that extends far beyond your lifetime.

Part 8: Investing in Yourself

Buying Knowledge: Education and Mentorship

Investing in yourself is arguably one of the most rewarding financial decisions you can make. Unlike material possessions, which depreciate over time, the knowledge and skills you acquire through education and mentorship continue to appreciate, often leading to opportunities that compound in value. Whether it's expanding your professional expertise, learning a new skill, or gaining insight into better decision-making, prioritizing personal growth lays a solid foundation for success. The benefits of such investments extend beyond professional achievements, influencing every facet of life—from increased confidence to more fulfilling relationships and enhanced resilience in the face of challenges. This ongoing commitment to self-improvement not only enhances your life but also empowers you to contribute meaningfully to your community and inspire others to embark on similar journeys.

One of the most effective ways to invest in yourself is by seeking high-quality education. This doesn't necessarily mean returning to formal schooling or pursuing degrees; instead, it involves strategically choosing courses, workshops, and programs that align with your goals. For example, an entrepreneur might benefit from taking a course in digital marketing to enhance their business's online presence. Similarly, someone looking to improve their personal finances might opt for a workshop on budgeting or investing. High-quality courses often provide structured content, expert insights, and actionable steps that accelerate your progress toward your objectives. These programs are not only about knowledge acquisition but also about empowerment—giving you the confidence to apply what you've learned in meaningful and transformative ways. Additionally, such courses often foster connections with peers and instructors, creating a network of support and shared growth.

The process of choosing the right educational opportunity involves a careful assessment of your goals and the resources available to you. Start by identifying the areas where you feel improvement is necessary or desirable. Do you need to refine your technical skills, deepen your understanding of a particular field, or develop your leadership abilities? Once you've defined your objectives, research programs that match these needs. Look for courses that emphasize practical application, as this ensures that what you learn can be immediately integrated into your personal or professional life.

Workshops and seminars are particularly valuable for those who thrive in interactive environments. These formats encourage active participation and often provide opportunities for hands-on learning. For instance, a workshop on time management might include real-time exercises to help you identify inefficiencies and develop strategies for improvement. Similarly, a seminar on public speaking might involve practice sessions where you receive immediate feedback, helping you build confidence and refine your approach. The insights gained from these experiences often stick with you longer than passive forms of learning, making them a worthwhile investment.

Books are another treasure trove of knowledge that should not be overlooked. For a relatively small investment, you can access the ideas and strategies of some of the world's greatest thinkers and achievers. Biographies of successful individuals, for example, can offer valuable lessons in resilience, creativity, and strategic thinking. These stories not only inspire but also provide actionable insights that you can apply to your own journey. Meanwhile, books focused on skill development, such as those on negotiation, emotional intelligence, or financial planning, equip you with tools that have both immediate and long-term benefits. The habit of regular reading fosters a mindset of continuous improvement, helping you stay adaptable in an ever-changing world.

For those seeking a more personalized approach, mentorship and coaching offer unparalleled opportunities for growth. Unlike self-directed learning, these relationships provide tailored guidance that addresses your specific needs and challenges. A mentor's role is to share their expertise and experiences, helping you navigate obstacles and seize opportunities with greater confidence. Similarly, a coach can help you set realistic goals, develop actionable plans, and stay accountable throughout the process. Both mentorship and coaching often accelerate your learning curve, allowing you to achieve results more efficiently than you would on your own.

One of the unique benefits of mentorship is the access it provides to the mentor's network and resources. A mentor's connections can open doors to opportunities you might not have discovered otherwise, while their insights offer a shortcut to understanding complex issues. Mentorship is not merely about receiving advice; it's a partnership built on trust and mutual respect, often leading to lifelong relationships that continue to add value over time. Coaching, on the other hand, is usually more structured, with a clear focus on measurable outcomes. A coach's expertise helps you identify blind spots, refine your strategies, and develop the skills necessary to overcome challenges effectively.

When deciding how to invest in your education and personal development, it's essential to evaluate the return on investment (ROI) for each opportunity. Consider not just the financial cost but also the time and energy required. Research the credibility of the program or individual offering the course or mentorship. Look for reviews, testimonials, and case studies that provide evidence of effectiveness. Programs that include practical components, such as projects or simulations, often deliver more value than those focused solely on theory. By carefully selecting opportunities that align with your goals, you ensure that your resources are spent wisely and yield meaningful results.

The benefits of investing in yourself extend beyond the tangible outcomes. Gaining new skills and knowledge enhances your confidence and broadens your horizons. It fosters a growth mindset—the belief that abilities can be developed through effort and learning. This mindset is invaluable in navigating challenges, as it enables you to view setbacks as opportunities for growth rather than as failures. Over time, this perspective transforms the way you approach both your personal and professional life, making you more resilient, innovative, and adaptable.

Moreover, self-investment often has a ripple effect on those around you. As you grow, you inspire others to pursue their own paths of development. Whether it's family members, colleagues, or friends, your commitment to improvement sets an example that encourages others to prioritize their growth. This collective culture of learning creates an environment where everyone benefits, fostering collaboration and shared success. By lifting yourself, you create opportunities to lift others, contributing to a cycle of mutual progress and empowerment.

Ultimately, investing in yourself is an act of self-empowerment that yields dividends far beyond financial gain. It signals a commitment to realizing your potential and living a life of purpose and fulfillment. Whether you're attending a workshop, reading a transformative book, or working with a mentor, these investments are a testament to your dedication to growth and excellence. By prioritizing your personal development, you position yourself for long-term success and create a foundation for a richer, more meaningful life. The journey of self-improvement is not a one-time effort but a lifelong pursuit that continually enriches both you and the world around you.

Books are another treasure trove of knowledge, offering limitless opportunities for learning and growth. For a relatively small investment, you can gain access to the minds of some of the world's greatest thinkers and practitioners. These repositories of wisdom allow you to explore diverse perspectives and ideas that challenge your thinking and broaden your horizons. Reading widely across subjects not only enhances your understanding of specific fields but also equips you with the ability to connect seemingly unrelated concepts, fostering creativity and innovation. Each book you read becomes a building block in a larger framework of knowledge, expanding your mental toolkit and enabling you to approach problems with fresh perspectives.

The value of books goes beyond their content; they serve as gateways to understanding the principles and methodologies of experts across a variety of disciplines. Biographies of successful individuals, for instance, reveal the persistence, failures, and strategies that shaped their journeys. These stories provide valuable insights into overcoming obstacles and achieving goals, often acting as a source of inspiration for readers facing similar challenges. Books on leadership, emotional intelligence, or financial literacy can equip you with practical tools and strategies to enhance both your personal and professional life. Whether it's mastering time management or understanding global economic trends, books have the power to transform your outlook and provide actionable knowledge that translates into measurable progress.

Reading isn't limited to passive consumption; it encourages active engagement. Taking notes, reflecting on ideas, and discussing concepts with others deepen comprehension and ensure long-term retention. Moreover, books often act as a catalyst for deeper exploration into subjects that pique your curiosity. A single chapter or insight can spark a lifelong interest, leading you to seek further education or develop expertise in a field. This cascading effect turns reading into a dynamic and evolving process of self-improvement.

For those seeking more interactive and personalized learning experiences, mentorship and coaching offer unparalleled opportunities for growth. Unlike books or courses, which provide generalized knowledge, mentorship is tailored to your specific needs and circumstances. A mentor's guidance can help you navigate complex decisions, identify opportunities for advancement, and avoid common pitfalls. Through regular feedback and encouragement, mentors foster accountability and accelerate your progress toward achieving your goals. Coaching, whether in a professional or personal context, provides actionable strategies designed to address immediate challenges while also building a foundation for long-term success.

One of the key benefits of mentorship is the access it provides to the mentor's network and expertise. A mentor's connections can open doors to opportunities that might otherwise remain out of reach, while their insights offer a shortcut to understanding nuances that could take years to learn independently. Mentorship is not just about receiving advice; it's about building a relationship based on trust, mutual respect, and a shared commitment to growth. Over time, this relationship evolves, often leading to collaboration and a deeper exchange of ideas.

Coaching, on the other hand, is often more structured and goal-oriented. A coach helps you set clear objectives, develop actionable plans, and measure progress along the way. This structured approach ensures that your efforts remain focused and aligned with your broader ambitions. Whether it's improving communication skills, developing leadership qualities, or overcoming personal barriers, coaching equips you with the tools and confidence needed to achieve transformative results.

When deciding how to invest in your education and personal growth, it's important to evaluate the potential return on investment (ROI) of each opportunity. Consider the time, money, and energy required and weigh these against the skills, knowledge, and connections you stand to gain. Look for programs and resources that align closely with your goals and values. High-quality courses, for example, often include hands-on projects or practical applications that reinforce learning and ensure that the knowledge gained can be readily applied in real-world scenarios.

Additionally, don't underestimate the importance of community in your learning journey. Joining study groups, attending workshops, or participating in online forums can enhance your understanding and create a support network of like-minded individuals. Engaging with others who share your goals not only deepens your learning but also fosters collaboration and accountability. These interactions often lead to the exchange of ideas and resources, enriching the learning experience and broadening your perspective.

Ultimately, investing in yourself is an act of self-empowerment. It signals a commitment to growth, resilience, and the pursuit of excellence. Whether you're delving into the pages of a book, seeking guidance from a mentor, or participating in a hands-on workshop, these investments pay dividends in both tangible and intangible ways. By continuously expanding your knowledge and skills, you position yourself for greater opportunities, increased confidence, and a richer, more fulfilling life.

Biographies of successful individuals, for example, can offer invaluable lessons in perseverance, strategy, and innovation. They provide a window into the thought processes, challenges, and breakthroughs of accomplished figures, enabling you to draw parallels to your own life and ambitions. By learning how these individuals overcame adversity and seized opportunities, you gain practical insights that can guide your journey toward success. Additionally, these stories often serve as powerful sources of motivation, reminding you that even the most celebrated achievements often come from humble beginnings and relentless effort. The lessons gleaned from these narratives can act as guideposts, helping you navigate your own challenges with greater clarity and determination.

Meanwhile, books focused on technical skills, leadership, or personal development are like tools in a well-stocked workshop, ready to help you tackle specific challenges and seize new opportunities. A book on coding, for instance, could teach you the fundamentals of a highly sought-after skill, while a leadership manual might provide strategies for effective communication and team management. Books on personal development, such as those addressing productivity or emotional intelligence, can transform the way you approach your daily life and interactions, fostering both personal and professional growth. A well-chosen book has the power to shift your mindset, inspire action, and provide a roadmap for achieving goals you once thought unattainable. The cumulative effect of consistently reading and applying knowledge is transformative, creating an ongoing cycle of learning and success.

For those seeking personalized guidance, 1:1 coaching sessions or mentorships can be transformative. Unlike generic advice, these interactions provide tailored feedback and actionable strategies designed specifically for you. A mentor or coach can help you identify blind spots, set achievable goals, and navigate obstacles with confidence. Their experience often accelerates your learning curve, allowing you to achieve results more efficiently than you would on your own. Additionally, mentorships often come with the added benefit of access to valuable networks and connections, further amplifying your opportunities. The value of mentorship lies not only in the advice received but also in the shared experiences and insights that guide you through your journey with clarity and purpose. The one-on-one nature of these interactions ensures that your unique challenges and aspirations are addressed, creating a deeply impactful learning experience.

Mentorship also fosters accountability. Having someone to regularly check in with can keep you focused and motivated to stay on track. This level of personal attention is difficult to replicate in self-directed learning and often makes the difference between stagnation and significant progress. Moreover, the relationships formed during mentorship often extend far beyond the initial arrangement, evolving into lifelong connections that continue to offer value over time. Mentors often open doors to opportunities you might not have considered or had access to, further enhancing the long-term benefits of their guidance.

However, not all educational investments are created equal. Evaluating what's worth your time and money is crucial to maximizing your returns. Begin by clearly defining your goals—what do you want to achieve, and how will this investment help you get there? Research the provider's credibility, the curriculum's relevance, and reviews from past participants to gauge whether the offering meets your needs. Look for programs or materials that emphasize practical application rather than just theoretical knowledge. For instance, a coding bootcamp that includes hands-on projects and real-world scenarios will likely provide more value than a course focused solely on lectures. The evaluation process ensures that your time, energy, and financial resources are directed toward endeavors that truly align with your aspirations. Investing wisely requires discernment and a commitment to aligning your efforts with your broader personal and professional goals.

Time is another factor to consider. Education and mentorship require a commitment of both money and time, so it's important to ensure the potential outcomes justify the investment. If a course or mentorship program aligns with your career or personal growth goals but requires significant time, weigh its long-term benefits against the short-term sacrifices. The key is to view time spent learning as an investment in your future self. Even when it requires prioritizing or reshuffling your schedule, the payoff in terms of skills acquired, opportunities unlocked, and confidence gained often far outweighs the initial sacrifices. By treating time as a resource, you cultivate discipline and intentionality, ensuring that every hour spent learning adds measurable value to your life. Additionally, this disciplined approach to time management often spills over into other areas of your life, enhancing productivity and focus.

Investing in your own knowledge also has intangible benefits that extend beyond career advancement. Gaining new skills boosts your confidence, broadens your horizons, and enhances your ability to adapt to change. It fosters a growth mindset—the belief that abilities can be developed through dedication and effort—which is invaluable in navigating life's challenges and opportunities. A growth mindset doesn't just prepare you to succeed; it equips you to learn from setbacks, turning obstacles into stepping stones toward greater achievements. This adaptability is crucial in an ever-evolving world, where staying stagnant can mean falling behind. The confidence gained through self-improvement radiates into all aspects of your life, enhancing relationships, decision-making, and overall satisfaction.

Moreover, the process of self-improvement has a ripple effect. As you grow, you inspire those around you to pursue their own paths of development. Whether it's family members, colleagues, or friends, your commitment to investing in yourself sets an example that can encourage others to prioritize their growth. This collective commitment to self-betterment fosters a culture of continuous learning and shared success, creating an environment where everyone benefits. By lifting yourself, you create opportunities to lift others, fostering an interconnected web of progress and mutual support. Your journey of self-investment becomes a source of inspiration, proving that the pursuit of knowledge and growth is a lifelong endeavor with endless rewards.

Ultimately, investing in yourself is an act of self-empowerment. It signals to yourself and others that you value your potential and are committed to realizing it. Whether it's purchasing a course, devouring books, or engaging with a mentor, these investments yield dividends not just in financial terms but also in personal fulfillment and growth. By prioritizing your own development, you position yourself for long-term success and create a foundation for a richer, more meaningful life. The impact of these investments extends far beyond the individual, shaping the lives of those you touch and contributing to a world where knowledge, skills, and passion are shared for the greater good. Each step you take to improve yourself is a step toward creating a legacy of continuous learning and enduring impact, a testament to the power of personal growth in transforming not only your own life but also the lives of others.

Part 9: Taking Action and Staying Disciplined

Turning plans into progress requires more than just determination; it demands a mindset rooted in consistency and a deliberate approach to achieving financial goals. While many begin their journey with ambitious plans, the real challenge lies in transforming those plans into tangible progress. This process is about cultivating habits, building resilience, and creating systems that keep you focused even when obstacles arise.

Achieving financial success is a journey, not a destination. To stay on course, it's crucial to break down lofty aspirations into smaller, manageable steps. Imagine setting a goal to save for a down payment on a home. The task can feel overwhelming until it is divided into actionable components: creating a realistic monthly budget, automating savings contributions, and identifying discretionary expenses to cut back on. Each of these small steps serves as a milestone, moving you closer to the ultimate goal and reinforcing the belief that success is within reach.

Consistency is a cornerstone of financial discipline. Establishing a routine tailored to your goals helps embed them into your daily life. For example, dedicating a specific time each week to review your finances—whether it's tracking expenses, assessing your progress, or planning upcoming expenditures—turns financial management into a habit. Over time, these consistent actions become second nature, making it easier to maintain momentum and achieve long-term objectives.

Setbacks are an inevitable part of the journey, but they do not have to derail your progress. Life is unpredictable, and unexpected expenses or financial missteps can happen to anyone. The key is to view these challenges as opportunities to learn and adjust. If you find that a particular budget isn't working, take a closer look at your spending habits and identify areas where changes can be made. Rather than dwelling on the setback, focus on the lessons it offers and use them to refine your strategy.

Building resilience is essential for navigating these inevitable challenges. Resilience isn't about avoiding difficulties but about facing them with determination and a problem-solving mindset. When financial setbacks occur, remind yourself that progress is rarely linear. Each challenge overcome is a step closer to mastery and success. Having an emergency fund in place, for example, can act as a financial cushion, offering peace of mind and the flexibility to handle unexpected costs without derailing your plans.

Motivation plays a pivotal role in maintaining discipline. One way to stay motivated is by reconnecting with the purpose behind your financial goals. Whether it's providing stability for your family, achieving independence, or pursuing a lifelong dream, keeping these reasons in mind provides a powerful source of inspiration. Visual aids, such as a vision board or even a list of affirmations, can serve as daily reminders of what you're working toward. These visual cues help sustain focus and reignite your drive during moments of doubt.

Celebrating progress is equally important. Reaching a financial milestone—no matter how small—deserves recognition. These celebrations act as positive reinforcement, making the journey more enjoyable and motivating you to continue. For example, after successfully paying off a credit card or reaching a savings target, reward yourself with something meaningful yet reasonable. These moments of acknowledgment not only boost morale but also reinforce the behaviors that led to the achievement.

Surrounding yourself with supportive individuals is another crucial factor in maintaining discipline. Sharing your financial goals with trusted friends, family members, or accountability partners creates a network of encouragement. This support system can provide perspective during setbacks and celebrate victories alongside you. Learning from others who have achieved similar goals can also offer valuable insights and strategies, showing you that success is attainable with persistence and the right approach.

To sustain progress, it's essential to establish systems that support your financial journey. Automation is one of the most effective tools for staying disciplined. Automatically transferring a portion of your income into savings or investment accounts ensures that these priorities are met without requiring constant effort or decision-making. Similarly, automating bill payments prevents missed deadlines and avoids unnecessary fees, preserving your financial stability.

Tracking progress is another vital system for success. Regularly reviewing your financial situation keeps you informed and allows you to make adjustments as needed. This practice provides a clear understanding of where you stand in relation to your goals, highlighting areas of improvement and celebrating accomplishments. Whether you use a simple spreadsheet, a financial app, or the guidance of an advisor, staying informed ensures that you remain proactive rather than reactive in managing your finances.

Creating a financial routine can also help you stay on track. Setting aside time each month to review your budget, analyze your spending, and reassess your goals creates structure and accountability. These regular check-ins allow you to adapt to changing circumstances while maintaining a clear focus on what matters most. A well-structured routine transforms financial discipline from a chore into a sustainable habit.

Long-term success requires patience and adaptability. Financial goals are often marathons rather than sprints, and it's important to remind yourself that meaningful progress takes time. Small, consistent actions accumulate over months and years, leading to significant outcomes. Just as compound interest grows exponentially over time, so too does the impact of disciplined financial habits.

As your life evolves, your financial priorities may shift. Periodically revisiting and refining your goals ensures that they remain aligned with your values and aspirations. A goal to save for a child's education may give way to a focus on retirement planning as your circumstances change. Embracing flexibility allows you to adapt while staying true to your overarching vision for financial security and fulfillment.

Taking action and staying disciplined isn't just about achieving financial milestones—it's about building a mindset and a lifestyle that supports long-term well-being. By transforming plans into progress, overcoming setbacks, and staying motivated, you lay the groundwork for a future defined by financial stability and personal satisfaction. The journey requires effort, but the rewards of financial freedom and peace of mind make every step worthwhile.

Part 10: Thriving in the Digital Financial Era

Staying Ahead in the Digital Age

In an era where almost every aspect of life has a digital counterpart, managing your finances is no exception. The convenience of online banking, digital wallets, and financial apps is unparalleled, but with this ease comes an increased responsibility to protect your financial data and assets. This chapter delves deeply into the essentials of cybersecurity and adapting to digital finance, ensuring you stay ahead in the rapidly evolving financial landscape.

Cybersecurity and Protecting Your Finances

Today's interconnected world offers incredible financial opportunities, but it also presents significant risks. Cyberattacks are becoming increasingly sophisticated, targeting individuals and organizations alike. Protecting your finances requires vigilance and a proactive approach to safeguarding your data.

Start by securing your online accounts with strong, unique passwords. A strong password should be a combination of uppercase and lowercase letters, numbers, and special characters. Avoid using easily guessed information like your birthday or common words. Better yet, use a password manager to generate and store complex passwords securely. This reduces the risk of reusing passwords across platforms—a common vulnerability hackers exploit. For added security, change your passwords regularly and avoid sharing them, even with trusted individuals.

Enable two-factor authentication (2FA) wherever possible. This adds an extra layer of security by requiring a second verification step, such as a code sent to your phone or email. Even if someone gains access to your password, 2FA makes it significantly harder for them to breach your account. Some systems also offer biometric options, like fingerprint or facial recognition, which can enhance your security even further. Biometric authentication, in particular, is becoming increasingly popular for its convenience and robustness, as it ties access to something uniquely yours, making it virtually impossible to replicate.

Additionally, many platforms now offer app-based authenticators, such as Google Authenticator or Microsoft Authenticator, as alternatives to SMS codes. These apps provide time-sensitive codes that are more secure than SMS, which can be intercepted by sophisticated attackers. Consider integrating these methods into your account security strategy for an added layer of protection.

It's also worth regularly reviewing and updating your 2FA methods. As technology evolves, new options emerge that may provide better security or convenience. Periodically check the settings on your accounts to ensure that your 2FA setup is both active and optimized. Remember, the extra effort you invest in enabling and maintaining robust authentication protocols significantly reduces your exposure to unauthorized access.

Be cautious of phishing attempts. Phishing scams often involve emails or messages that appear to be from legitimate institutions, tricking you into revealing sensitive information. Look for red flags such as misspelled domains, urgent language, or requests for passwords or financial details. Always verify the source before clicking on links or sharing information. Phishing schemes are increasingly sophisticated, with attackers sometimes using personalized details to seem credible. Staying vigilant is your best defense.

Regularly monitor your accounts for suspicious activity. Most banks and financial institutions offer real-time alerts for transactions. Enabling these notifications ensures you're immediately aware of unauthorized activity. If you notice anything unusual, report it to your bank or financial provider without delay. Additionally, periodically review your account statements and credit reports to spot any discrepancies early.

Invest in antivirus and antimalware software to protect your devices. These tools help prevent malicious software from infiltrating your systems, safeguarding sensitive data. Keep your software updated to ensure you're protected against the latest threats. Additionally, avoid using public Wi-Fi for financial transactions, as these networks are often unsecured and vulnerable to hackers. If you must use public Wi-Fi, consider employing a virtual private network (VPN) to encrypt your connection and shield your data from prying eyes.

Educate yourself about the latest scams and threats. Cybersecurity is an ever-evolving field, and staying informed is one of your best defenses. Follow trusted cybersecurity sources, attend webinars, or even take online courses to deepen your understanding of protecting your digital assets. Awareness is critical, as new schemes and vulnerabilities emerge regularly. By staying informed, you're better equipped to recognize and avoid potential risks.

Adapting to Digital Finance

The rise of digital finance has revolutionized how we manage, save, and invest our money. Platforms like online banks, robo-advisors, and mobile payment apps have made financial management more accessible and efficient. However, adapting to these technologies requires a balanced approach that embraces innovation while staying mindful of potential risks.

Begin by exploring digital banking options. Many online banks offer lower fees, higher interest rates on savings, and user-friendly platforms compared to traditional banks. However, it's essential to research the institution's security measures and reputation before making the switch. Look for banks with robust encryption, 2FA, and reliable customer support to ensure your money is secure. Additionally, check if the bank is insured by a reputable regulatory body to protect your deposits in case of unforeseen circumstances.

Financial apps can be powerful tools for budgeting, investing, and saving. Apps like Mint, YNAB (You Need A Budget), and Acorns help you track spending, automate savings, and even round up transactions to invest spare change. When choosing an app, review its security features and read user reviews to ensure it aligns with your financial goals. Many apps now integrate artificial intelligence to provide personalized recommendations, making it easier to optimize your financial strategies.

Cryptocurrency and blockchain technology represent some of the most significant advancements in digital finance. While these innovations offer exciting opportunities, they also come with considerable risks. Before investing in cryptocurrencies, take the time to understand how they work, the volatility of the market, and the security measures needed to protect your assets. Use reputable exchanges and consider storing your crypto in a hardware wallet for added safety. Diversify your investments within the crypto space, and never invest more than you can afford to lose, as the market remains highly unpredictable.

Embracing digital finance also means staying agile and adaptable. The financial landscape is evolving rapidly, and keeping up with new technologies is crucial. Follow financial news, participate in online forums, and engage with thought leaders in the fintech space to stay informed about emerging trends. This proactive approach helps you identify opportunities and avoid pitfalls as the industry continues to innovate. Staying ahead means being willing to experiment with new tools while maintaining a cautious, well-informed perspective.

Online trading platforms and robo-advisors are also gaining popularity, offering cost-effective ways to manage investments. These platforms use algorithms to create personalized portfolios based on your risk tolerance and financial goals. While convenient, it's important to review their methodologies and ensure they align with your investment philosophy. Combine the efficiency of robo-advisors with occasional reviews from human financial advisors for a well-rounded approach.

Finally, maintain a healthy skepticism of new technologies or platforms that promise high returns with minimal risk. Scams often exploit the allure of easy money, so always do your due diligence before investing or sharing financial information. Trustworthy platforms are transparent about their operations and provide clear, verifiable information. Always verify the credibility of any platform or app, and consult with trusted professionals if you're unsure about its legitimacy.

By mastering cybersecurity and leveraging the advantages of digital finance, you can confidently navigate the digital era. The key is to strike a balance between embracing innovation and protecting your assets, ensuring that you remain secure and successful in an increasingly connected world. The future of finance is digital, and with the right tools and mindset, you can thrive in this exciting and transformative landscape.

Conclusion: Your Journey Ahead - Time to Level Up

As you turn the final pages of this book, it's time to take a moment and reflect on the journey you've undertaken. You've explored the nuances of financial realities, from breaking free of paycheck-to-paycheck cycles to mastering the art of investing and building wealth. Along the way, you've uncovered strategies, learned from stories, and been armed with tools to create the life you've always envisioned. But now comes the most important part—action.

Financial success isn't about perfection. It's about progress. It's not measured by how quickly you reach your goals but by the consistency and determination with which you pursue them. Every choice you make, no matter how small, is a step forward. Whether it's saving an extra £50 a month, investing in your first index fund, or choosing to spend your money in alignment with your values, each decision is a brick in the foundation of your financial freedom.

Think back to the concepts you've learned throughout this book. You've mastered the art of distinguishing between assets and liabilities, learned how to avoid common financial pitfalls, and uncovered the power of compounding. You now understand that wealth isn't reserved for the privileged few—it's attainable for anyone willing to take charge of their financial destiny. These lessons have equipped you not only with the tools to navigate your financial future but also with a renewed sense of empowerment and control over your life. You've learned to view money not as an obstacle or a source of stress, but as a tool—one that, when used wisely, can unlock a world of possibilities and create opportunities beyond what you may have imagined.

Reflect on how far you've come in redefining your relationship with money. The knowledge you've gained isn't just about numbers; it's about reshaping your mindset and embracing a perspective of abundance and possibility. You've learned that financial freedom is not built on a single monumental act but through consistent, intentional decisions made over time. Each concept you've explored in this book serves as a stepping stone, guiding you toward a life where you are in control of your choices and future.

Consider the practical applications of what you've absorbed. Whether it's understanding how to leverage the power of compounding through strategic investments, identifying and nurturing assets, or making informed decisions that align with your values, these tools are your keys to unlocking financial security and independence. The confidence you've built in navigating complex financial topics empowers you to take decisive action, turning dreams into tangible outcomes.

More importantly, these lessons have illuminated that wealth isn't confined to bank accounts or investment portfolios. True wealth encompasses the freedom to pursue passions, the security to weather life's uncertainties, and the ability to give back in meaningful ways. This holistic view of prosperity transforms your financial journey from a pursuit of material gains into a pathway toward personal fulfillment and impact.

Let this realization be your foundation as you forge ahead. Money, when understood and managed with intention, becomes a means of liberation rather than limitation. The possibilities before you are limitless, and the power to create the life you desire lies firmly in your hands. With every decision you make, you're not just managing resources—you're shaping a legacy that extends beyond your lifetime, influencing those around you and inspiring future generations.

Reflect on the journey you've undertaken to reach this point. Each chapter of this book has built upon the last, forming a cohesive roadmap to financial freedom. The insights gained aren't just theoretical; they're practical, actionable steps that can be applied in your daily life. Whether it's understanding the importance of an emergency fund, demystifying the stock market, or learning how to spot financial opportunities others might overlook, these concepts are designed to empower you to take the reins of your financial destiny.

More importantly, this book has shown you that financial freedom isn't an exclusive club. It's not about luck or inherent privilege but about deliberate choices and consistent effort. It's a journey that anyone can embark on, regardless of their starting point. Wealth is no longer an abstract dream; it's a tangible, achievable goal within your reach. And perhaps the most profound realization is that the journey doesn't just transform your finances—it transforms you. By taking control of your money, you're also reclaiming control of your time, your opportunities, and your future.

Let this knowledge be your foundation as you move forward, a constant reminder that the power to change your financial narrative lies in your hands. The journey ahead is yours to shape, and the possibilities are limitless.

But knowledge alone is not enough. True transformation happens when you apply what you've learned. Start small, but start today. Begin by reviewing your financial reality. Where are you now, and where do you want to be? Break down your goals into actionable steps and set realistic timelines. Remember, the journey to financial freedom is not a sprint but a marathon. Celebrate your progress along the way, and don't let setbacks deter you. They are merely detours, not dead ends.

One of the most powerful lessons from this journey is that you have the ability to create a legacy. Whether it's leaving behind financial security for your family, contributing to causes you care deeply about, or simply living a life free from financial stress, the choices you make today ripple far beyond your immediate future. You are not just building wealth; you are creating possibilities—for yourself, for your loved ones, and for your community.

As you continue your journey, remember the importance of adaptability. The financial landscape will change, and so will your circumstances and priorities. Stay curious, keep learning, and remain open to new opportunities. Personal growth and financial growth are intertwined, and investing in yourself is one of the best decisions you can make. Seek out mentors, surround yourself with supportive individuals, and don't be afraid to ask questions or pivot when necessary. Success is not linear, but with perseverance, it is inevitable.

Finally, embrace the possibilities that financial freedom can bring. Picture the life you want to lead. What does it look like? What does it feel like? Hold onto that vision as you move forward. Let it be the fuel that drives you through the challenges and the reward that awaits you on the other side. Financial freedom isn't just about money; it's about choice, empowerment, and the ability to live life on your own terms.

Your journey is just beginning, and the best is yet to come. You have everything you need to succeed: the knowledge, the tools, and the mindset. Now it's time to embrace this new chapter with determination and confidence. The road ahead may be long, but every step you take will bring you closer to the future you've dreamed of. It's not just about achieving milestones—it's about building a life defined by purpose, freedom, and fulfillment.

Think of this moment as the turning point where preparation meets opportunity. You've equipped yourself with the skills to navigate challenges, the wisdom to make informed decisions, and the courage to take calculated risks. Each choice you make—from investing in your education to setting long-term financial goals—is an affirmation of your commitment to growth and success. Don't underestimate the power of incremental progress; even the smallest actions can yield extraordinary results over time. Each step you take, no matter how minor it may seem, builds upon the last, creating a ripple effect that compounds into significant achievements. It is in these consistent, focused efforts that true progress lies.

This is your moment to redefine what's possible. The work you've done so far has laid the foundation for a future of endless potential. By embracing the principles of patience and persistence, you're setting yourself up for sustainable success. Remember, the journey isn't about perfection; it's about resilience. Challenges will come, and mistakes may happen, but it is your ability to adapt and learn from these experiences that will set you apart. Each obstacle overcome strengthens your resolve, making you more prepared for the opportunities that lie ahead.

Take a moment to envision where you want to be five, ten, or even twenty years from now. Picture the life you're building and the freedom you're creating—freedom to make choices without the constraints of financial stress, freedom to spend your time on what matters most, and freedom to give back in ways that inspire others. This vision is not just a dream; it's a blueprint, and each action you take today brings you one step closer to turning it into reality.

You have already proven your ability to grow, learn, and rise to the occasion. Now, let this turning point serve as the catalyst for even greater achievements. Your financial journey is more than a series of numbers or milestones; it's a testament to your determination, your courage, and your belief in what's possible. So, take the next step with confidence and know that the future you're striving for is well within your reach.

The path to financial freedom is filled with opportunities to learn, grow, and redefine what's possible. Along the way, you'll encounter moments of doubt, frustration, and even setbacks, but these are the experiences that will shape your resilience and fortify your resolve. Each challenge faced is a lesson learned, teaching you something new about your capabilities and your capacity to overcome adversity. These moments are not barriers but stepping stones—opportunities to recalibrate, rethink, and rise stronger.

Embrace these challenges as intrinsic parts of your journey, not as signs of failure but as milestones of progress. Reflect on each obstacle as it arises, and ask yourself what it's teaching you about your goals, your methods, or even your motivations. Are you pushing yourself to grow in ways you hadn't imagined? Are you learning new strategies to adapt and overcome? These moments of introspection are invaluable, offering insights that refine your approach and clarify your path forward.

Each challenge you overcome is more than a task checked off a list—it's a story of growth, resilience, and perseverance. These trials test your limits, yes, but they also reveal your potential. They teach you that success isn't about avoiding difficulty but about rising to meet it, learning to navigate through it, and emerging stronger on the other side. Each setback you turn into a stepping stone builds your confidence and reinforces the belief that you are capable of achieving the extraordinary.

This process of navigating difficulty is what ultimately transforms dreams into reality, laying the groundwork for a life of resilience, adaptability, and fulfillment. Every detour or hurdle is an opportunity to reassess your values and reaffirm your commitment to your vision. It is through this relentless determination and willingness to persevere that you create a life not just of success but of deep, lasting significance. Challenges, after all, are not the barriers to your journey—they are the journey itself, the trials that shape your story and define your legacy.

Remember, financial freedom isn't just about accumulating wealth; it's about creating choices. It's the ability to decide how you want to spend your time, who you want to spend it with, and what legacy you want to leave behind. By taking control of your financial destiny, you're not only transforming your life but also inspiring those around you to strive for their own potential.

So, take that first step today. Whether it's crafting a new budget, starting your investment journey, or simply committing to lifelong learning, every action brings you closer to your vision. The journey to financial freedom is yours to claim, and the possibilities are boundless. Go out there and own it with confidence, passion, and purpose.

Conclusion: Thank You and Looking Ahead

Thank you for choosing this book and taking the time to invest in your financial future. Writing this was not just about sharing knowledge; it was about empowering you to take charge of your journey and achieve the life you've always envisioned. The fact that you've reached this point demonstrates your commitment to growth, and that's a powerful first step. You've proven that you have the drive to create positive changes, and that determination is the foundation of every great achievement.

The road ahead is filled with opportunities, challenges, and discoveries, but every step forward brings you closer to your goals. Embrace the uncertainties and celebrate the victories, both big and small. Each decision you make, no matter how minor it seems, plays a vital role in shaping your financial journey. Whether you're starting with small adjustments, like budgeting or saving, or diving into significant transformations, such as investing or starting a business, remember that progress is what truly matters. The journey to financial freedom is as much about the process as it is about the destination. Celebrate your milestones with pride, learn from your setbacks with grace, and never lose sight of your vision for the future.

I hope this book has provided you with the tools, insights, and inspiration to take action and thrive in your financial journey. The future is bright, and it's yours to shape with purpose and determination. You have the knowledge to make informed decisions, the ability to adapt to changing circumstances, and the resilience to overcome any challenges that come your way. Financial success is not just about wealth; it's about the freedom and security to live the life you desire. Now, it's time to take what you've learned and make it your own, crafting a path that reflects your values and aspirations.

As you move forward, remember that you're not alone on this journey. Countless others are walking similar paths, striving to achieve their dreams and create a better future. Share your experiences, inspire those around you, and continue to seek out opportunities for growth and learning. Your actions not only impact your life but also have the potential to inspire and uplift those who look to you as an example of what's possible.

Thank you once again for allowing me to be a part of your journey. It has been an honor to guide you through these steps and to provide insights that can make a meaningful difference in your life. Here's to a future filled with possibilities, freedom, and success. Your dedication, resilience, and courage are what make this journey extraordinary. You've got this—and the best is yet to come.

Printed in Great Britain
by Amazon